詠春拳全集

詠春拳歷史與傳統紀實

COMPLETE WING CHUN

詠春拳全集
詠春拳歷史與傳統紀實

COMPLETE WING CHUN

THE DEFINITIVE GUIDE TO WING CHUN'S HISTORY AND TRADITIONS

Robert Chu
Rene Ritchie
Y. Wu

Disclaimer: Please note that the publisher and author(s) of this instructional book are NOT RESPONSIBLE in any manner whatsoever for any injury that may result from practicing the techniques and/or following the instructions given within. Martial Arts training can be dangerous—both to you and to others—if not practiced safely. If you're in doubt as to how to proceed or whether your practice is safe, consult with a trained martial arts teacher before beginning. Since the physical activities described herein may be too strenuous in nature for some readers, it is also essential that a physician be consulted prior to training.

First published in 1998 by Tuttle Publishing, an imprint of Periplus Editions (HK) Ltd., with editorial offices at 153 Milk Street, Boston, Massachusetts 02109.

Copyright © 1998 Robert Chu, René Ritchie, Y. Wu

All rights reserved. No part of this publication may be reproduced or utilized in any form or by any means, electronic or mechanical, including photocopying, recording, or by any information storage and retrieval system, without prior written permission from the publisher.

Library of Congress Catalog Card Number: 98-060626

ISBN: 0-8048-3141-6

Distributed by:

North America
Tuttle Publishing
Distribution Center
Airport Industrial Park
364 Innovation Drive
North Clarendon, VT 05759-9436
Tel: (802) 773-8930
Fax: (802) 773-6993
Email: info@tuttlepublishing.com
Web site: www.tuttlepublishing.com

Japan
Tuttle Publishing
Yaekari Building, 3rd Floor
5-4-12 Ōsaki, Shinagawa-ku, Tokyo
Japan 141-0032
Tel: (03) 5437-0171
Fax: (03) 5437-0755
Email: tuttle-sales@gol.com

Asia Pacific
Berkeley Books Pte. Ltd.
130 Joo Seng Road
#06-01/03 Olivine Building
Singapore 368357
Tel: (65) 6280-3320
Fax: (65) 6280-6290
Email: inquiries@periplus.com.sg

Indonesia
PT Java Books Indonesia
Jl. Kelapa Gading Kirana
Blok A14 No. 17
Jakarta 14240 Indonesia
Tel: (62-21) 451-5351
Fax: (62-21) 453-4987
Email: cs@javabooks.co.id

First edition
08 07 06 05 04   7 6 5 4 3

Printed in the United States of America

DEDICATION

We dedicate this book to our Wing Chun ancestors who passed this great system down to us, and to our fellow Wing Chun kuen practitioners who keep the art alive today.

TABLE OF CONTENTS

Foreword by Mark V. Wiley ix

Acknowledgments xi

Introduction 1
Notes on Genealogy 2
Notes on Language 2

1. Yip Man Wing Chun 4
History and Development 4
Basic Movements 10
Forms and Training 13
Concepts and Principles 23
Conclusion 27

2. Yuen Kay-San Wing Chun Kuen 28
History and Development 28
Basic Movements 32
Forms and Training 34
Concepts and Principles 43
Conclusion 44

3. Gu Lao Wing Chun Kuen 45
History and Development 45
Basic Movements 47
Forms and Training 47
Concepts and Principles 51
Conclusion 52

4. Nanyang Wing Chun Kuen 53
History and Development 53
Basic Movements 56

Forms and Training 60
Concepts and Principles 65
Conclusion 68

5. Pan Nam Wing Chun Kuen 69
History and Development 69
Basic Movements 73
Forms and Training 73
Concepts and Principles 76
Conclusion 77

6. Pao Fa Lien Wing Chun Kuen 78
History and Development 78
Basic Movements 80
Forms and Training 81
Concepts and Principles 82
Conclusion 82

7. Hung Suen Wing Chun Kuen 83
History and Development 83
Forms and Training 85
Concepts and Principles 88
Conclusion 89

8. Jee Shim Wing Chun Kuen 90
History and Development 90
Basic Movements 94
Forms and Training 95
Concepts and Principles 97
Conclusion 99

9. Other Wing Chun Kuen Styles 100
Fujian Wing Chun Kuen 100
Hung Suen Hay Ban Wing Chun Kuen 100
Malaysian Wing Chun Kuen 101
Pien San Wing Chun Kuen 102
Vietnamese Wing Chun Kuen 103
Yiu Kai Wing Chun Kuen 104
Other Branches 104

Conclusion 106
Stage 1, Predecessors of Wing Chun 106
Stage 2, Founders of Wing Chun 109
Stage 3, Red Junk Ancestors of Wing Chun 115
Stage 4, Disseminators of Wing Chun 117
Stage 5, Developers of Wing Chun .118
Final Thoughts 120

The Wing Chun Kuen Family Tree 122

Glossary 124

About the Authors 143

FOREWORD

I began the study of Wing Chun kung-fu at the age of sixteen. I was already a black belt in taekwondo at the time, and involved in the study of escrima and arnis, but felt an inexplicable attraction to the art by the legacy left behind by the late Bruce Lee. The first book I ever read on the martial arts was Dan Inosanto's *Jeet Kune Do: The Art and Philosophy of Bruce Lee*. After reading this book and about the training methods and fighting art of Lee, I knew that if I wanted to become as good as Lee I would have to study the arts he did. As I read on, I discovered that Wing Chun was the nucleus of his new style.

Fifteen years later, I am still interested and intrigued by this compact martial art system. I never actually perfected or completed the system as a result of poor scheduling (spreading myself too thin among different arts), and moving from place to place. However, I was exposed to the Yip Man system as taught by William Cheung and Moy Yat, and the Jun Fan (Bruce Lee) Wing Chun system as taught by Dan Inosanto and his students.

Over the years I have read several articles about Wing Chun systems not associated with the art's legendary master, Yip Man. To my surprise, I discovered that there are actually several lineages of this economical art form, with variations among the forms and in their respective training methods. After reading these articles my interest again peaked. Sadly, however, there was no substantial information on the topic available to the uninitiated.

While working as the martial arts editor for Tuttle Publishing in Tokyo in 1996, I received a package from their United States office in Boston. It was a manuscript on the art of Wing Chun by Robert Chu, Rene Ritchie, and Y. Wu, with a big rejection notice on it. Since Tuttle already had three books on the subject, and there are dozens of Wing Chun books on the market, the company didn't think there was a need for the book. I, too, didn't think this would be much different than a brief history of Yip Man and an overview of the three base forms. To my surprise after scanning the table of contents, however, I discovered that there was much more to this book—and art—than I had initially assumed or ever expected. I immediately contacted the authors and contracted their book.

The authors have successfully traced the lineages and history of eight Wing Chun styles and present them here as the masters of the respective arts have passed them down through oral traditions. This is particularly insightful as it not only presents many points of view on a variety of topics—such as the real meaning of the term Wing Chun—but stays true to the teachings and traditions of each system by the authors not adding in their own thoughts. All of this information is then presented side-by-side for the interested reader to cross check and make his own decision as to what he chooses to believe and how he then interprets the art form. Given their in-depth research into the many Wing Chun systems, the authors then draw together the various oral histories with fact and construct, in the Conclusion, what they believe to be the actual history and development of the art and its many collateral systems. A detailed Glossary is also presented, with the corresponding Chinese characters for further reference and interpretation.

Wing Chun instructors (left to right) Robert Chu, Mark Wiley, Hawkins Cheung, Gary Lam.

Complete Wing Chun is perhaps the best book written on the various schools comprising a single martial art form. The authors have done an excellent job in their tireless research and presentation of material into this comprehensive treatise on one of the most controversial and misunderstood arts of this century. This book is destined to become the classic reference on the subject, and has set a standard by which other researchers and practitioners wishing to uncover their art should follow. I highly recommend this book to all Wing Chun stylists and martial arts researchers alike without hesitation. If ever you were to buy just one book on the art, this should be it.

—Mark V. Wiley

ACKNOWLEDGMENTS

The authors would like to thank Mark V. Wiley for recognizing and believing in the potential of this work. Eddie Chong, sifu of Pan Nam Wing Chun, for sharing his knowledge, and John Murphy and Garrett Gee, sifu of Hung Suen Wing Chun, for contributing their chapter. Also, many thanks to Jane Hallander for her photographs of Pao Fa Lien Wing Chun, Reiner Klimke and Andreas Hoffman sifu for their notes on Jee Shim Wing Chun (Chi Sim Ving Tsun), Ilya Olshanetsky and Andrej Moskwitin for their notes on Vietnamese Wing Chun (Vinh Xuan), and Y. C. Yeung for his kind help on several of the branches of Wing Chun. The work would have been considerably lessened without their generous contributions. Thanks as well to the Internet Wing Chun Mailing List, created and maintained by Marty Goldberg and Robert Gillespie, an outstanding forum for exchange among Wing Chun practitioners (information on the WCML can be obtained by sending e-mail to majordomo@efn.org with the message body reading: info wingchun).

Robert Chu would like to thank Hawkins Cheung, Kwan Jong-Yuen, William Cheung, Koo Sang, Augustine Fong, Eddie Chong, Eric Kwai, Jeung Ma-Chut, Gary Lam, Johnny Wong, Allan Fong, Henry Moy and the Moy Yat Wing Chun family for sharing their Wing Chun. Special thanks to his students and good friends who have taught him as much as he taught them, James Ng, Stephen Eng, Anant Tinaphong, all his New York students, and all his Los Angeles students, especially, Stephen Wenger, Patrick Lee, Dimitris Horiatis, Robert Ting, David Young, and Peter Kwong who have supported him over the years. Also special thanks to Robert S. Weinberg Sensei for starting him on the path to martial arts and his brothers, Charles, Johnson and Douglas Chu, who kept him inspired. Also special thanks to his two partners and sworn brothers, Rene Ritchie for sharing with him his Yuen Kay-San Wing Chun kuen, and to Ng Yew-Mun, who shared his Nanyang Wing Chun kuen on his brief visit. It was their urging that led him to the completion of this project despite his dislike for rewrites. He couldn't ask for two better partners. Most of all, special thanks to his beautiful wife, Pauline, for putting up with mistress Wing Chun for all these years.

Y. Wu would like to thank and express his appreciation for the years of friendship and knowledge from Victor Leow of the Intelligent Combative Arts Network Australasia, his sworn senior kung-fu brother, mentor, and above all teacher (and author of *Virtual, Intelligent, Kinaesthetically Oriented Geometric Articulations (VIKOGA): Authenticated Mindwill Wing Chun Gungfu*). Thanks also go to big brother Robert Chu for generously sharing his knowledge of Wing Chun kuen; brother Rene Ritchie for his Yuen Kay San Wing Chun kuen and vast knowledge of the history of Wing Chun kuen; sifu Hawkins Cheung for his entertaining and highly knowledgeable views on the application of Yip Man Wing Chun kuen and the Wing Chun *baat jaam do,* and Gary Lam for his insights into the late Wong Shun Leung's methods. Special thanks to Yap Boh Lim, S. Y. Liu, Leong Lin Heng, Beh Lau Seng and Hui See Lim, all great teachers from various martial arts traditions who have contributed to his knowledge. In addition, thanks to his student Long Tian Ching for his photography and Alan Ang who started him on the Internet and keeper of the Nanyang Wing Chun Website at http://sunflower.singnet.com.sg/~angalan. Last but not least, many thanks to his wonderful one in a million wife Alice for her tolerance, understanding and love.

Rene Ritchie would like to thank his teacher, Ngo Lui-Kay (Ao Leiqi) for sharing with him grandmaster Sum Nung's teachings of Yuen Kay-San's art and for his continual support, encouragement, and assistance with this project and others. In addition, thanks to his classmates Antony Casella, Georgia Dow, David Johnson, Deon Weir, and Wilson Woo for all their assistance. Also, thanks to Yuen Jo-Tong, Y. C. Yeung, Dan Lam, Bud Shapard, and Michael Engle of the Yuen Kay-San style and to Jim Roselando and the many other Wing Chun enthusiasts he has had a chance to converse with over the years.

Thanks also to Kenny Fung for his help with Chinese language and culture. Lastly, special thanks to his co-authors and big martial brothers Robert Chu and Y. Wu for sharing with him their knowledge and widening his understanding of the many branches of the art.

INTRODUCTION

前言

When Bruce Lee first exploded on television and into the movies, he captured the imagination and hearts of people all over the world. With the fame of Bruce Lee, the conditions in Hong Kong, and the hard work and effort of many of his classmates, the Wing Chun of his teacher, Yip Man, became one of the most well-known and popular Chinese martial arts in the world. Although this gave Wing Chun international recognition, it also led to a lot of misconceptions. Due to a lack of authentic information, many mistakenly came to assume that the renowned Yip Man was the sole inheritor of the style and that his Wing Chun was the lone version of the art.

In fact, there are several different and distinct systems of Wing Chun. Unfortunately, over the years most of these systems have remained unseen or unreported to all but a few. From where then do these misconceptions come?

Over time, Wing Chun's history has become a mishmash of factual accounts and fictionalized stories. Early secrecy and modern marketing did much to create and fuel the confusion. Legendary figures like Ng Mui and Yim Wing-Chun are believed to be the sole founders of the art and a single lineage through Leung Bok-Chao, Leung Lan-Kwai, Wong Wah-Bo, and Leung Yee-Tai to Leung Jan has become accepted as the only branch.

The doors of Wing Chun, however, were never this closed, nor the line this limited. Over the generations, many highly skilled masters of the past have learned the art, contributed enormously to its development, and passed along their knowledge. Yet, masters such as Cheung "Tan Sao" Ng and many of the Red Junk actors like Dai Fa Min Kam, Gao Lo Chung, Hung Gan Biu and their descendants have disappeared entirely from all but a very few records.

As Wing Chun's origins and development have remained relatively unknown, so has its true breadth. Inside the Bamboo Curtain of the People's Republic of China, however, many branches including the Yuen Kay-San, Gu Lao, Pao Fa Lien, Jee Shim, Pan Nam, Hung Suen,

Pien San, and even the early Foshan students of Yip Man survived the rise of communism and the Cultural Revolution. While the Yip Man style was brought to Hong Kong around 1950, the Yuen Kay-San, Pao Fa Lien, Pien San, and Jee Shim styles followed soon thereafter. Beyond China, Wing Chun spread into Southeast Asia over half a century ago and today many unique versions of the art can be found in Singapore, Malaysia, Vietnam, and surrounding areas.

Thus, it has been very difficult to find real information on the Wing Chun family of styles, especially in the western world.

Complete Wing Chun, presents, for the first time, seldom seen information on over a dozen branches of the Wing Chun art. It is hoped that this volume will serve as a helpful resource for the interested newcomer and as a valuable reference for the long-time enthusiast.

NOTES ON GENEALOGY

Wing Chun kuen, while a relatively young style by Chinese martial arts standards, is one which has grown much since the mid-1900s, and one which has, unfortunately, been plagued by more then its share of controversy. Thus, the history of Wing Chun's founding (who created the style) and development (who passed the art along to whom) presented in this book is not, and cannot, be exact.

Over the generations, due to errors, omissions, mix-ups, padding, filling, and modification, many different genealogies have come to exist for the same style or individual. In addition, since some practitioners had more then one teacher, and some also studied with grand-teachers, senior classmates, friends, and so on, the lines and stories are sometimes quite muddled, with different branches recording different aspects.

For the purposes of this book and out of respect for the various branches, the following chapters present the history of the different arts as their masters orally transmit them. While some of these accounts may appear similar and in some cases repetitive, it is necessary in order to properly present the history and traditions of each branch.

It is not our goal to promote one style over another and while we do present our own thoughts in the conclusion, we encourage the readers to consider them all, and to decide for themselves. In our humble opinion, each holds but a piece of the puzzle.

NOTES ON LANGUAGE

The modern origins of Wing Chun kuen can be traced back to the Guangdong province of southern China. Guangdonghua

(Cantonese), the language spoken there, is the mother tongue of Wing Chun and hence the dialect in which we present the historical and technical names in this book. Names of places are given in the official People's Republic of China dialect and romanization, Mandarin pinyin, since that is how they are rendered on most modern maps.

While Mandarin has the increasingly popular pinyin method of romanization, there is no such standard for Guangdonghua. Due to this fact, over the years, many different English "spellings" have been devised to render the terms of Wing Chun. To simplify things for this book, we have explored many of the different popular romanizations, and chosen those we felt best rendered the sounds involved.

To help eliminate confusion, the glossary at the end of the book will present Cantonese and pinyin romanizations, traditional Chinese characters, and English translations.

CHAPTER 1

YIP MAN WING CHUN

Yip Man Wing Chun, the first system of Wing Chun kuen to be taught publicly has become one of the most popular Chinese martial arts in the world today. The modern history of Wing Chun (also commonly romanized as Ving Tsun and Wing Tsun by many of Yip Man's descendants), began with the changes wrought by the Communist takeover in 1949. With his property and wealth taken from him under the communist regime, Grandmaster Yip Man fled China and came to Hong Kong. Yip Man's misfortune, however, became the free world's blessing, for soon after arriving in Hong Kong he began his career as a professional martial arts instructor.

HISTORY AND DEVELOPMENT

The legend of Wing Chun begins in the Qing dynasty with the Siu Lam Jee (Shaolinsi or Young Forest Temple). The Siu Lam Temple offered not only religious sanctuary but also a safe house from the military hunting for anti-Qing revolutionaries. It was only a matter of time, however, before the Manchurians made the decision to eradicate this source of rebellious activity. With the treacherous aid of Siu Lam insiders such as Ma Ning-Yee, the Qing troops laid siege to the temple from without, while the temple was burned from within. Siu Lam was laid to waste. Out of the conflagration, the *ng jo* (five elders) of Siu Lam fled and went into hiding. The five elders consisted of Jee Shim Sim Si (Jee Shim, Chan Buddhist Teacher), Fung Dao-Duk, Miu Hin, Bak Mei Dao Yan (White Eyebrows, Taoist), and Ng Mui Si Tai (Five Plums, Nun). Ng Mui (Wu Mei) fled to the Bak Hok Jee (Baihesi or White Crane Temple) on the slopes of the Daliang Mountains. There, on the border of Sichuan and Yunnan province, legend states Ng Mui witnessed a fight between a crane and a snake. Inspired by the encounters, she combined the animals' movements with her own Siu Lam boxing and created the principles of a new, as yet unnamed, martial art.

Since the art was intended only for those loyal to the Ming throne, it was taught in secrecy and to just a few carefully selected students. Ng Mui eventually took on a female disciple, Yim Wing-Chun and taught her this unnamed system. Yim was known for her beauty and cunning and was desired by a local ruffian who tried to force her into marriage. Using the art taught to her by Ng Mui, Wing-Chun challenged and defeated her unwelcome suitor, driving him from the area and firmly establishing her reputation as a fighter.

Yim Wing-Chun later married her betrothed; a salt merchant named Leung Bok-Chao. Yim passed the martial art of Ng Mui on to her husband, who named it Wing Chun kuen (Wing-Chun's Boxing) in her honor. From Leung Bok-Chao the style passed on to Hung Suen (Red Boat) Opera member, Leung Lan-Kwai (although some legends state that Leung was a wealthy scholar or Chinese herbalist). Leung Lan-Kwai passed the art to Wong Wah-Bo and Leung Yee-Tai, also of the Red Boat Opera.

A picture of Grandmaster Yip Man seen in many of the schools descending from his teachings.

Legends hold that Leung Yee-Tai was a poler for the Chinese Opera troop, whose job it was to steer the boat away from rocks or shallow water by pushing off with a long pole. On the boat, Leung befriended a cook who was really Jee Shim, the former abbot of the Siu Lam Temple in hiding. Jee Shim decided to teach Leung the famous six-and-a-half point pole set and its applications. Leung soon mastered the techniques and later he met another martial artist named Wong Wah-Bo, a master of Wing Chun kuen. They became close friends and discussed the principles of their martial arts. The two decided to trade and share their knowledge. After much refinement, the six-and-a-half point pole was

The Ving Tsun Athletic Association, the nexus for Yip Man's art in Hong Kong.

incorporated into the Wing Chun curriculum.

Both Wong Wah-Bo and Leung Yee-Tai taught the notable Dr. Leung Jan of Foshan who brought fame to Wing Chun through his exploits, many of which have since been romanticized into stories and movies.

Dr. Leung Jan, a noted local herbalist, was known both as Jan Sin-Sang (Mr. Jan) for his professional and gentle nature and also as Wing Chun Wong (King of Wing Chun) for his fighting prowess and fierce reputation in challenge matches. Leung Jan taught at his store Jan Sang Tong (Mr. Jan's Hall) on Fai Jee Street in Foshan and had a number of students, among them his own sons Leung Chun and Leung Bik, and his disciple, Chan Wah-Shun.

Chan Wah-Shun, often called Jiao-Chin Wah (Moneychanger Wah) due to his profession as a currency converter, proved himself outstanding in the practice of Wing Chun. A large and powerful man, Chan carried on his teacher's reputation in challenge matches, and enhanced Wing Chun's reputation in Foshan with his victories.

Among Chan Wah-Shun's disciples (said to have numbered sixteen in all) were his son, Chan Yiu-Min, and students Ng Siu-Lo, Ng Jung-So, Lui Yiu-Chai, Lai Hip-Chi, and Yip Man, among others.

It was Yip Man, Chan Wah-Shun's final disciple, who went on to change the history of Wing Chun forever. Born in the mid-1890s to a wealthy family in Foshan, at roughly the age of thirteen (although some accounts suggest earlier) Yip Man approached Chan Wah-Shun, who taught on the Yip family's property, and sought instruction. Chan, at first, thought the young Yip Man was too scholarly and gentle for the martial arts. Hoping to dissuade the young man, Chan asked Yip for a substantial tuition. Yip's desire was so great, however, that he returned immediately with his life's savings, intent on pursuing lessons. Yip Man's dedication won over Chan and he accepted Yip as his last disciple. A short time later, when the old moneychanger passed away, Yip Man continued his lessons under Ng Jung-So, one of Chan's most senior and talented disciples.

One account holds that Yip Man came to learn Wing Chun again while in Hong Kong attending school at St. Stephen's college during the 1910s. Through a classmate, Yip was introduced to an old man who was said to be skilled in the martial arts. Yip, known for his brash and feisty character, challenged the old timer. According to some accounts, Yip charged at the old man, missed, and fell into the water at the pier where the match was taking place. Yip Man later found out the old man was, in fact, Leung Bik, the son of Leung Jan and his own *sibak* (martial arts uncle). Suitably impressed, Yip followed Leung Bik for the next few years, polishing his Wing Chun before making his way back to Foshan.

In those days, it was not uncommon for practitioners of Wing Chun to keep their knowledge secret, and simply not teach at all. So it was that, at first, Yip Man himself did not teach and practiced only with his good friends and martial arts peers. During the Japanese occupation, conditions changed. Life grew more difficult and Yip saw his wealth and prosperity dwindle. In 1941, to repay the kindness of Chow Chen-Chung, Yip Man taught some students in the nearby village of Yongan. These pupils included Chow's son Kwong-Yiu, as well as Kwok Fu, Chan Chi-Sun, Lun Kai, and Chow Sai. As of this writing, most of Yip Man's early 1940s students have passed away. Kwok Fu and Lun Gai, however, still preserve his art in Foshan.

If nothing had changed, Yip Man probably would have remained in Foshan and Wing Chun would likely never have attained the fame it currently enjoys around the world.

The winds of change, however, soon swept over China in the form of Mao Zedong's Communist Party seizing power in 1949, after the defeat of the Nationalists and their retreat to Taiwan. Under Communist rule, Yip Man lost his wealth and property and had no choice but to flee his homeland.

In late 1949, fate brought Yip Man once again to Hong Kong. No longer young or wealthy, Yip took shelter at the Restaurant Workers Association in Kowloon, to which he was introduced by his good friend Lee Man. Teaching at the association at the time was a man named Leung Sheung. Although Leung Sheung taught Choy Lay Fut, he had also been exposed to lung ying mor kiu (dragon-shape rubbing bridges style), Bak Mei pai, and the Jee Shim Wing Chun of Dong Suen. Age had not dampened Yip Man's feistiness and, according to one account, he critiqued Leung's performance rather sarcastically in front of his class. Yip's slight build emboldened the larger Leung Sheung. Leung threw down his challenge, the end result of which saw Leung asking to become Yip Man's disciple and Yip starting his career as a professional Wing Chun teacher in Hong Kong.

Masters Wong Shun-Leung and Hawkins Cheung, two of Yip Man's students who helped forge Wing Chun's reputation in challenge fights.

In the spring of 1950, Yip began with just over a dozen students. A short time later another class commenced with well over two dozen students. By 1951, a third class had begun with over forty people. Wing Chun proliferated among the restaurant workers and its reputation had spread, attracting people from outside the association as well. Wing Chun was finally taught publicly after decades of secrecy.

The early years saw the rise of Yip Man's reputation as a teacher and that of Wing Chun as a fighting art. Yip's students issued and accepted many challenges. Yip Man taught literally thousands of students over the years hailing from varying social classes. Among his followers were his senior disciples who helped him instruct, a group of high school students, professionals, Restaurant and Bus Driver Association members, and more affluent private pupils.

Master William Cheung is based in Australia and teaches internationally.

Some of Yip Man's early disciples included Leung Sheung (famous for his *biu jee* set), Lok Yiu (famous for his Wing Chun pole), Tsui Seung-Tin (famous for his *siu nim tao* set), and Wong Shun-Leung (famous for his application of Wing Chun in challenge matches and street fights).

Through their victories in challenge matches, Wong Shun-

Leung, Cheung Chuk-Hing (William Cheung, now in Australia and teaching internationally through his World Wing Chun Kung Fu Association), Lee Siu-Lung (Bruce Lee, who more than anyone else helped popularize and spread Wing Chun and kung-fu in general around the world through his movies and teachings), Cheung Hok-Kin (Hawkins Cheung, now teaching in Los Angeles, California), and others firmly established Wing Chun's reputation as a fighting art in Hong Kong.

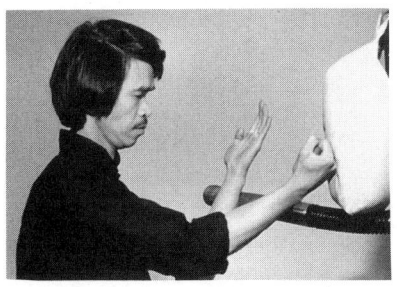

Master Hawkins Cheung shows an example of simultaneous attack and defense.

Yip Man also passed along his art to his family members, including his nephew, Lo Man-Kam (now in Taipei, Taiwan) and his sons Yip Chun and Yip Ching when they later left Foshan for Hong Kong in 1962.

Other Wing Chun practitioners from Yip Man's lineage who were responsible for spreading the art include Wang Kiu in Europe, Kan Wah-Chit (Victor Kan) in the United Kingdom, Leung Ting teaching around the world through his International Wing Tsun Martial Arts Association, Lee Shing in England, Ho Kam Ming teaching in Macao and Canada, Fung Hon (Stewart Fung) in Canada, Chan Shing (Chris Chan) in San Francisco, Moy Yat in New York, Leung Siu-Hung (Duncan Leung) in Virginia, Fong Chi-Wing (Augustine Fong) in Arizona, Chung Man-Lin (Ken Chung) in San Francisco, Chong Yin-Cheung (Eddie Chong) in Sacramento, Yeung Biu (Robert Yeung) in Hawaii, and many, many others.

Master Leung Ting is the leader of the International Wing Tsun Martial Arts Association.

In 1972, after having passed along his Wing Chun to thousands of students, and seeing the art spread around the globe, Grandmaster Yip Man passed away as a result of complications from throat cancer.

Although at times politics, rivalry, controversy, and some

Five instructors of wing Chun in the Los Angeles area: (left to right) Jim Lau, Hawkins Cheung, Robert Chu, Gary Lam, Jerry McKinley.

infamy have surrounded Yip Man's art, the style itself has made great strides forward. It is hoped that remaining differences will be resolved and that the Yip Man family will continue on in harmony, proudly claiming its place as one of the most popular forms of Chinese martial arts practiced around the world.

BASIC MOVEMENTS

Yip Man's Wing Chun basics stress the fundamental structure with the *yee jee kim yeung ma* and the three essentials of *tan sao, bong sao*, and *fook sao*.

The *yee jee kim yeung ma* (goat clamping stance), also known as the "inward rotation abduction stance," trains stability, force redirection and projection, and is the basic stance and structure of the system. Structure refers to the positioning and form of the body, stance, waist, and hands in order to connect the body and maximize power to the limbs. In Yip Man Wing Chun, the waist and pelvis push forward upon receiving pressure. If the waist and pelvis are not pushed forward, the upper torso will collapse when pressure is received, thereby breaking the structure. Weight is distributed evenly between both legs and the buttocks are ahead of the rear heel. *Yee jee kim yeung ma* is also the root of the other stances and steps in the system, including *bik ma* (pressing step), *chum kiu ma* (seeking bridge horse, the sideways facing stance from the second set), *kao bo* (hooking step), *sam gwok ma* (triangle step), *gwok ma* (angle step), and *juen ma* (turning step). In general, these stances emphasize a 50/50 weight distribution, although some Yip Man Wing Chun instructors vary this in their teachings. During *bik ma* stepping or in the *juen ma* turning stance, when pushed, the rear leg has the feeling of being pushed into the ground and when pulled, the forward leg has a feeling of being pulled into the ground. This gives the practitioner the sense of being firmly rooted to the earth.

In recent years, there has been some disagreement over the nature and form of footwork in Yip Man Wing Chun, becoming a noted source of controversy. However, it is known that Yip Man taught his students various methods of stepping while either dragging or picking up the feet, in both fixed and relaxed stances.

Tan sao (spread-out hand) is the basic configuration from which the other arm shapes are derived. *Tan sao* faces ninety-degrees perpendicular to the body and its height is determined by facing the opponent or by the "bridge" (extended arm) it comes in contact with. The hand is straightened out and the wrist is bent naturally. *Tan sao* also trains the *hei* (*qi*, internal energy) circulation and force projection. An old Wing Chun saying holds that "under heaven the *tan sao* is invincible," and it is known that when Yip Man practiced the first set, *siu nim tao,* he would spend at least an hour on the *tan sao* section.

Bong sao (wing arm) is probably the trademark of Wing Chun, so unique and outstanding is its shape. In the *bong sao,* the forearm indicates a gradual dip

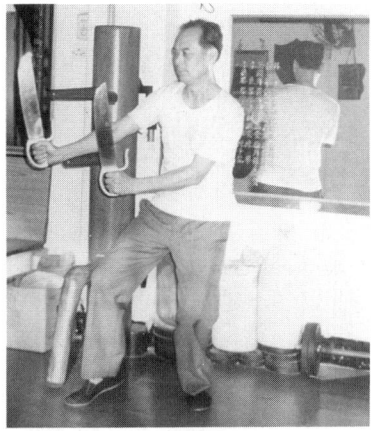

Master Koo Sang practices a movement from the *baat jaam dao*.

Gaun Gwun from the *luk dim boon gwun* techniques is demonstrated by Master Koo Sang.

and the shoulder is kept relaxed. It is the only core Wing Chun hand position in which the elbow flies outward. The technique varies in height according to the opponent's attacking bridge and its variations include high, middle, and low positions. *Bong sao* can only be executed when there is a force sufficient to create its need. When used, it can be employed as a shield, as a transitional move, or to slow or drag an opponent's attack. The dual nature and multidimensional aspects of the technique allow for vast differences in its interpretation. The traditional saying that "*bong sao* does not remain" serves to remind the practitioner that this technique must be used only in the moment of its need, then changed immediately.

Figure 1

Fook sao (subduing hand) is so-named after its design, which makes it ideal for subduing the force of an opponent's arm upon contact. Etymologically, the Chinese character for *fook* signifies a dog held down by a person, and this is exactly what the *fook sao* does through control of an opponent's leverage point. *Fook sao*, like *tan sao*, is also held perpendicular to the body. Its difference lies in that *fook sao* is an on-top-of-the-bridge position, whereas *tan sao* is a relatively underneath-the-bridge position. *Fook sao* arguably has the most transition positions and can lead into *lop sao* (grabbing hand), *gum sao* (pinning hand), *pak sao* (slapping hand), *jut sao* (choking hand), and other techniques (Figs. 1–3).

Figure 2

Figure 3

Master Hawkins Cheung squares off with his opponent (Fig. 1). As the opponent punches, Cheung Sifu moves in quickly, intercepting with his forearm (Fig. 2) and flowing straight into a counter strike (Fig. 3).

Tan sao, bong sao, and *fook sao* are the most important hand maneuvers in Wing Chun and are often thought of as fixed techniques. In actuality, however, they are very much alive and adaptable. The names are merely convenient terms for the ideal positions of the bridge arms in relation to an opponent. Since their feeling is alive, they only exist when in contact with an opponent and only for the time it takes to actually perform them in transition.

FORMS AND TRAINING

Yip Man's Wing Chun contains three empty hand forms that capture the core skills that define the art of Wing Chun.

It is interesting to note that while different branches of Yip Man Wing Chun all teach forms that follow the same basic principles, there is a great deal of variation in the sequences themselves. Perhaps Yip Man learned different variations from his different instructors, continuously strove to refine and improve his art throughout his teaching career, taught the sections with emphasis on conceptual points rather than fixed sequences, tailored the sets to suit each individual student, or the sets have simply been changed by current-day instructors to fit their own needs. Of course, mistakes, misunderstanding, and misinterpretation may have also led to such variation. In the end, it is not important which variation of the set is the "original," but rather that these sets give the practitioner a feel for the system's concepts, tools, and the basic knowledge necessary for their application.

Siu nim tao (little idea), the first form, is meant to give beginners an idea of the scope of Wing Chun techniques. Broken down, *siu* refers to "small, efficient, without waste, or compact and economical." *Nim* is "to immerse yourself in the study of a subject." Finally, *tao* refers to the "head." Together, *siu nim tao* can give the cryptic message of "put it in your head to study the concept of efficient, small, economical, compact motions." It is a training form, rather than a fighting form, emphasizing awareness of the centerline and the development of stance, body structure, and hand structure. Economy of motion is stressed, no excessive movement is required to deliver power to any of the "weapons" (i.e., attacking limbs) and when striking, the limbs do not vibrate. Basic offensive and defensive movements, centerline facing, proper elbow positioning for power, forward "spring" power, hands in coordination and independent of the body, development of sensing mind intention, and *hei (qi)* flow are also trained through *siu nim tao*. During the set, breathing is natural and the eyes follow the hands while peripheral vision is used to see in all directions. The mind is calm and as the name of the set implies, "don't have big ideas, just maintain a little idea." *Siu nim tao* has different levels of training and seeks to instill in practitioners important movements that are crucial to mastering the art. It is for this reason that *siu nim tao* is at once regarded the most basic yet most advanced form in the system.

Chum kiu (seeking bridge), the second form, refers to the timing of entry. Through the practice of the *chum kiu* set, practitioners learn to "seek when to bridge the gap between themselves and their opponents." The form teaches to close the distance with a bent arm,

(Fig. 4) The opponent faces Master Hawkins Cheung. (Fig. 5) As the opponent begins a front kick, Cheung Sifu immediately moves in.

(Figs. 6–8) Jamming the attack with a kick of his own, Cheung Sifu sends his opponent flying.

then to straighten the arms (e.g., strike) after entering. It requires footwork movements in all directions, with the body facing the opponent's centerline. The key idea of *chum kiu* is to break the opponent's body and defensive structure. It exemplifies the control of the bridges of the opponent and the significance of the Wing Chun body structure in motion. It shows the importance of maintaining the shifting and the turning of the stance, and rooting into the ground, not just spinning on the surface like a top. *Chum kiu* also develops good grounding and side stepping to cut off an opponent's circling movements. Through *chum kiu*, practitioners are trained in kicking, the high, middle, and low *bong sao*, the *lan sao* (obstructing arm), the *chou chui* (bouncing fist), and other tactics. The form teaches how to take and change the centerline and use it while moving; how to explode one's power with coordination between torso, waist, and stance; how to step through an opponent; and how to come into proper fighting range. In some respects, *chum kiu* can be considered the most advanced form in Wing Chun kuen (Figs. 4–8).

Biu jee (darting fingers), the third form, refers to the darting or thrusting motions trained in this set. *Biu jee* is comprised of the words *biu*, to "dart in," and *jee*, to "point at" (with a finger or compass needle). In essence, it means that a practitioner must "dart in at what they are facing." *Biu jee* trains an exponent in adjustments of position in relation to an opponent *(bien jung sien)* and stance. It comprises ways to break through an opponent's centerline, and emergency techniques which can be used to free a practitioner when they are trapped or their structure is broken. *Biu jee* also teaches to strike with the fingers at the body's weak points and develops one's bridges to become as hard as steel. In addition, the form includes hooking steps and shifting along three centerlines. As it was traditionally taught only to disciples, there is a saying that *"biu jee but chut mun"*(*biu jee* does not go out the door.) As Chinese characters have different meanings, this saying can have several interpretations: 1) Don't teach outsiders this set; 2) Don't use biu jee (darting fingers technique) outside of your gates; 3) Don't go out the door using biu jee. The question is which gate/door? *Biu jee* is only a secret, however, if one is unaware of its inner workings and understands the techniques solely on a superficial level.

Muk yan jong (wooden man dummy) is the only form in Wing Chun to be trained using an external aid. Contrary to its use in many styles of martial arts, the Wing Chun wooden dummy is not meant to be a device for toughening the arms. Rather, the dummy is used to help the practitioner to further understand concepts such as proper positioning and diffusion of force. Every section of the *muk yan jong* set is a means to check for proper body structure and stance. Bridges should stick to the dummy arms. The *muk yan jong* is taught in several stages. The first two sections of the set are the most important, with the remainder of the set being an artistic representation of the style. Typically, Yip Man would introduce the first two sections to a student, and the students would learn the rest of the set from their *si hing* (seniors). The *muk yan jong* has the most variation in the system, and may be due to this manner of teaching.

Basics on the wooden man dummy allow a student to do repetitious excerpts from the forms and practice these movements by themselves. They can practice *gaun sao* (cultivating hand), *kwun sao* (rolling arm), *huen sao* (circling arm), *seung fook* (double subduing arm), and *seung tok* (double lifting arm), among others, as drills on the device (Figs. 9, 10).

The *muk yan jong* set varies from 108 to 116 movements and from student to student. Typically, the sequence of the first sixty movements is performed virtually identically among each of Yip Man's students, whilst the remaining motions vary among the disciples. With the set, practitioners learn how to adjust their steps, develop power and closing skills, take the "proper" line, and how to use hand/foot combinations.

Practice of the *da san jong* (free-style dummy) encompasses breaking the set down into its applications in setting-up an opponent and the proper context in which to do so. Practitioners learn to juxtapose the sequence to develop their minds to vary and spontaneously change their tactics as needed.

Hong jong (air dummy) practice involves doing the set in the air, without the physical dummy, and allows the practitioner to learn to combine techniques, flow freely, and later to "shadow box."

The use and applications of the movements or *mai sang jong* (making the dummy come to life), involves practicing the techniques of the dummy set against a live partner.

Luk dim boon gwun (six-and-a-half point pole) consists of the seven underlying conceptual principles *tai* (raise), *lan* (obstruct), *dim* (point), *kit* (deflect), *got* (cut down), *wun* (circle), and *lao* (receive). The last principle is considered a half-motion as it allows one to withdraw the pole and start a new movement.

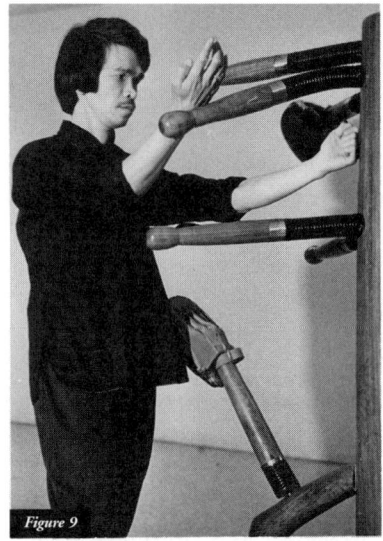

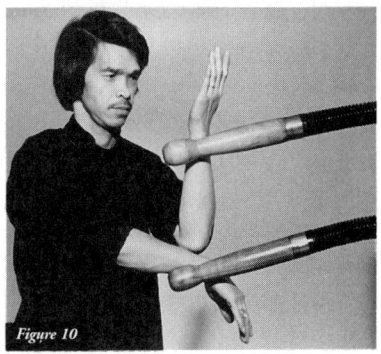

Master Hawkins Cheung practices *tan da* and *gaun sao* on a *muk yan jong*.

Many Yip Man Wing Chun practitioners prefer to explain the concepts in Wing Chun terminology using *biu* (dart), *tan* (spread-out), *bong* (wing), *fook* (subdue), *jut* (choke), *gaun* (cultivate), and *huen* (circle). Combined with stepping, angling, sensitivity, and interpreting energy, in addition to methods of issuing strength, these basic concepts may be combined to form innumerable permutations.

Historically, the pole was the shaft of the spear typically used by Chinese foot soldiers during times of war. Measuring seven to nine feet in length, it is thicker at the butt and tapers down to one inch in diameter at the tip. The pole is a heavy weapon and requires a practitioner to utilize correct body connection, body structure, and position.

Wing Chun pole training is based on the Siu Lam *luk dim boon gwun*. The original sequence has been simplified and shortened, training has been modified to include both the left and right hand lead positions, the grip has been reduced to match the shoulder width of the practitioner (and if one's standard is high, this distance is maintained while practicing with the pole), and *chi gwun* (sticking pole) has been introduced into the curriculum. An advanced practitioner can wield the long pole as if it were a toothpick. This is to say, one does not use the pole as if it were a heavy, long weapon, but rather a light, maneuverable weapon (Figs, 11–19).

Figure 11

Opening move for the 6 1/2 point pole.

In addition to the strengthening exercises and the pole form itself, there are a variety of supplemental drills which can be performed with the pole. One such drill involves affixing a small ball on a string as a target and repeatedly trying to strike the ball while it is stationary and while it is in motion. Another accuracy drill involves hitting coins or nuts or other small objects placed on the ground. Later, as a practitioner becomes more proficient, a spontaneous or live form is used and the practitioner can wield the pole in all eight directions. The front hand allows for front power and agile movement. The rear hand is the stabilizer for driving strength. The qualities of stabbing and thrusting, striking and cutting, jabbing and driving are combined and their attributes developed for application.

Figure 12

Saat gwun, a quick, downward stroke to an opponent's hand.

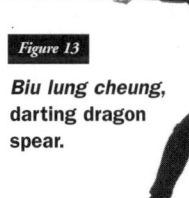

Figure 13

Biu lung cheung, darting dragon spear.

Once these drills are mastered, a student can move on to the *chi gwun* or sticking pole exercise. In this exercise, practitioners come into contact with and stick to each other's pole. Similar to sticking hands, the practitioners circle, position, and re-position to exploit the openings in each other's defense. Control is

Figure 14

Tiu gwun, jumping upward staff.

emphasized for if one thrusts or strikes too hard injuries can easily happen. *Chi gwun* exercises develop sensitivity through the pole, long distance positioning, and train stance, torso, and bridges. After one is proficient in *chi gwun,* a practitioner can move on to free-style sparring practiced slowly at first and then faster.

The most important principles when facing pole against pole is the Wing Chun saying, *"gwun mo leung heung"* (the pole has not two sounds). When using the pole, a practitioner should strike in one motion, hence, make one sound. The most efficient way to do this is by combining offense and defense in one motion. This does not mean first engaging a pole and then sliding down to strike the hand, for that makes two sounds. Rather, one should strike the hand immediately upon facing an opponent.

Figure 15
Dang gwun, hammering staff.

Baat jaam dao (eight slash knives) provides training in mobility and further enhances precision in movement. It is also excellent for training the waist to lead the body. The *baat jaam dao* is often considered the most advanced form in the Wing Chun system. It was, and still is, treated as such a secret that to this day only a few dedicated students are taught the knife set, if at all. It is a practical form devoid of fancy moves like flipping the knives backwards or twirling about in circles, and it stresses the footwork required in the Wing Chun system. It is said in Wing Chun circles that *"dao mo seung faat,"* which means the moves of the knives are not repeated. Imagine that a Wing Chun practitioner can injure or kill an opponent in one move, attack and defend simultaneously, and efficiently economize his motion. If one can picture that, one can have an idea of how the *baat jaam dao* streamlines the Wing Chun practitioner's ability and skill.

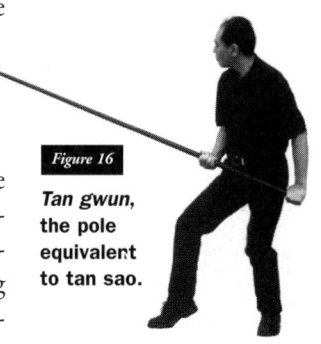

Figure 16
Tan gwun, the pole equivalent to tan sao.

There are several opinions as to why the double knife set is called the baat

Figure 17
Lou suei gwun, flowing water staff.

18

jaam dao. Some state that there are eight special slashes which include: *jut* (downward slice), *pek* (chopping), *jaam* (slashing), *waat* (sliding), *biu* (stabbing), *lao* (stirring), *chai* (stamping), and *huen* (circling), that comprise the set. Others hold that there are eight sections to the form. It is said that originally the Wing Chun knives were called the *yee jee seung dao,* owing to the fact that each section closed with a movement in which the parallel positioning of the knives made it look like the Chinese character for *yee* and that it was Yip Man himself who renamed the techniques *"baat jaam dao"* to give them a more conceptual label.

Figure 18
Fook gwun, subduing staff.

Some sharpen the skills of the knives on the wooden dummy. One must also sharpen the knife skills while striking objects. The knives are overall very simple in their application; as they touch, they injure. The *baat jaam do* train the armed application of Wing Chun principles, develop the bridge for breaking the centerline, train footwork, move to the outside gate, develop power, and develop the "butcher mind set" (an analogy of unrelenting cruelty to the opponent) (Figs. 20–31).

Figure 19
Lan gwun, the obstructing pole.

As Yip Man preferred to teach the practical, rather than have students memorize numerous keywords, he taught the essentials of his system through various basic partner exercises.

Pak sao (slapping hand) is the main defense against a fast strike. *Pak sao* is used to check the opponent's incoming blow and as a basis for follow-up to "capture the timing" of the opponent's movement and to initiate a counter-attack. Two partners train the exercise in *yee jee kim yeung ma,* with one partner doing *lien wan chui* (chain punches) and the other defending with *pak sao.* The eyes must follow the incoming blows, and particular attention must be paid to the torso and stance. With this exercise, a practitioner develops timing, hand and eye coordination, balance, and forward power with the *pak sao* and *chung chui* (thrusting punch).

Lop da (grab and strike) is important in teaching the student the use of the *bong sao* as a detaining technique, and the use of a grab and strike as a follow up. It is practiced with two partners in *yee jee kim yeung ma,* with one partner beginning the cycle with a *chung chui* and the

Figure 20
The low *sup jee dao* movement in the opening of the 8 slash knives set.

Figure 21
Upper crossed knives movement.

Figure 22
Chit dao, slicing knife.

Figure 23
Biu dao, darting knife.

Figure 24
Yee jee dao, parallel obstructing knives.

Figure 25
Tan Jaam Dao, dispersing and slashing maneuver.

other receiving with a *bong sao*. The *bong sao* is then followed with a *lop sao chung chui* combination which the first partner receives with a *bong sao*. The cycle is then continued numerous times and one may switch sides. There are many variations of *bong sao lop da*. A practitioner may vary the exercise with a push with *bong sao*, a step back and pull with *lop sao*, or changes with the attacking "weapon." With this exercise, one develops the "jerking power" to knock an opponent off balance, timing, coordination, the feeling of sticking to an opponent, how to follow up

Bong dao, wing knife.

Kwun dao, a combination of tan and bong knife.

Gaun dao, cultivating knife.

Tan dao/wang chit, dispersing knife and horizontal slash.

Jaam dao, slashing knives.

Biu dao, darting knife.

when an opening is made, and the hands to assist and follow each other.

Dan chi sao (single sticking hands) is a basic exercise which teaches the changes of *tan sao, bong sao,* and *fook sao.* This exercise can be varied with the positions of running up and down the bridge of the opponent. *Dan chi sao* makes defenses strong; develops proper positioning of *tan sao, bong sao,* and *fook sao;* develops timing while sticking; develops stance and structure; and develops proper elementary defense for *chi sao.*

Luk sao (rolling hands) is a maneuver designed to develop a student's sensitivity. *Luk sao* is the backbone of *chi sao*. Students learn to maintain the structure and stance during the *luk sao* exercise and vary the pressure (i.e., light vs. heavy), and the "running" of the hands. Mastery of running of the hands is important in learning how to cross the bridges. *Luk sao* develops the four major gate positions, which allow partners to create a bridge and the feeling of intention in the bridges. One develops proper coordination between *tan sao, bong sao, fook sao,* and the clean flow of techniques.

Seung chi sao (double sticking hands) is a drill in which the elements of Wing Chun are taught in a living laboratory or clinic. Through *luk sao,* students can learn to apply the movements taught in the three empty-hand sets and the wooden man set. It is known that when Yip Man taught *chi sao,* his students would always be gently falling backwards or forwards and unable to control their center of gravity. Yip Man would constantly have the students up on their heels or on the balls of their feet, while controlling their every movement. Some sources mention that Yip Man never bothered to touch hands with his students. This gave a great insight into the character of Yip Man. If he liked a student, he would do *chi sao* with them; if he didn't, he would pay no attention to them.

In *chi sao,* it is most important that the student learn to control his opponents' bridges and to set them up for the next shot. With *chi sao,* a practitioner learns to strike when an opponent's intention is not there, and to stay wary and mindful of one's own situation; to recognize opportunity, and become sensitive to it; the three major components of tools, timing, and positioning; and lastly, experience. Experience gives one the ability to recognize other avenues when before there seemed to be none. Advanced practitioners will practice *chi sao* while blindfolded, and with all the empty-hand tools, including the hands, feet, knees, elbows, and head. *Chi sao* practice helps to merge concept with practice. Often, students are advised: *"Chi sao mo lien fa sik"* (There are no flowery techniques in sticky hands practice"). *Chi sao* is the means to develop the most efficient way to strike an opponent. To utilize fancy techniques is to waste time and render the techniques inefficient.

Chi gerk (sticking legs) is a study by some of Yip Man's students on developing sensitivity with the legs. The principles of the Wing Chun hands also pertain to the legs. For example, the "asking hand" and "guard hand" techniques become the "asking foot" and "guard foot" techniques, and *tan sao, bong sao,* and *fook sao* can be done with the legs as well.

Chi gerk training allows one to isolate leg training and to develop balance, endurance, and tactile sensitivity with them. During *chi gerk* practice, one discovers that each step in Wing Chun is a potential kick. *Chi gerk* also teaches to alternate the legs, to trap an opponent's kick, and to "kick at the post" (e.g., attack the opponent's supporting leg). It develops whole body coordination and combinations of hand and foot techniques. It trains the mind to subconsciously react with feeling; and to develop the balanced use of fifty percent hands and feet. Yip Man Wing Chun has the saying *"gerk mo hui faat"* (the kick does not miss), which means to kick only when necessary and when one knows that it will score.

San sao (free fighting) trains the applications of Wing Chun techniques. *San sao* training gives the student a way to customize their own Wing Chun, develop confidence in their abilities when facing an opponent, and explore how to take the correct angle of entry.

CONCEPTS AND PRINCIPLES

Wing Chun is a martial art that is based on principles and concepts rather than just techniques alone.

Jung sien dui ying (centerline facing principle), also commonly referred to as the saggital plane, central line, mother line, middle line is the cornerstone principle of Wing Chun. By adhering to the centerline principle, the Wing Chun practitioner has occupied the optimal position from which to defend or attack. Thus, the centerline principle forms the basis for the study of proper positioning. By positioning and correctly aligning the anatomical tools in the centerline, the manifestation of power and force is maximized. Finally, the centerline principle defines the effective limit and the power path of each movement, and the areas protected by conceptual shielding.

The "principles of the centerline" include the fastest line of entry between two opponents. Yip Man Wing Chun utilizes it for simple, direct, economical motion and for non-telegraphic attacks. The optimal path to minimize the distance between striking weapon and target is a straight line. By dominating the sagittal plane, the opponent is forced to move along the perimeter of a circle where the Wing Chun practitioner in its center. Thus, any movement that the opponent initiates has to travel along a curved path and consequently takes longer to reach its target. By moving along the linear path, however, a practitioner can reach the opponent faster. Yet, in actual application, the linear is merged with the curved to generate a more powerful force through strong structure. There are several principles of the centerline in combat application, including:

- "Facing the centerline," or face an opponent "nose-to-nose," to control or occupy the centerline.

- "Controlling the centerline" involves maintaining and occupying the centerline with the stance and bridges, and not letting the opponent get out of control.
- "Changing the centerline" deals with when an opponent controls or occupies a practitioner's centerline, the practitioner merely changes to another angle of attack or changes his reference point minutely.
- "Returning to the centerline" relates to the concept of "changing the centerline," if an opponent takes control of the centerline, one must fight to regain it.
- "Breaking the centerline" comes into play when an opponent occupies the centerline, and one can smash or destroy his control. This is also a method of "changing the centerline," where one forcefully gains or regains control.
- "Mental centerline" shows that in Wing Chun, the word "centerline" not only refers to fighting but to one's mind, the things one does, the problems one solves, the life on lives. If one strays too far to the right or left, it takes some time to come back to the center. The center has no opinion. It is a way of looking at life, similar to Confucian *jung yung* teachings, the "middle Way" of Buddhism, or the going with the flow of Daoism. The centered mind is to see clearly. In life, one's yin and yang must be balanced for one to be in the center. One also looks at both sides of an issue, noting pros and cons of each. When one looks at an opponent, one is not looking to see his technique, but to see his mind and intention.

Bik ging (crowding power), also known as constant forward pressure, is another important concept. In Wing Chun, one wants to constantly pressure one's opponent by crowding an opponent's motions. The practitioner seeks to not give an opponent the chance to fully extend his blows, or let his blows reach maximum power and extension. An opponent's space is eaten up as if the practitioner were an amoeba. When an opponent retreats an inch, the Wing Chun fighter advances a mile. When the opponent's back is up against a wall, the Wing Chun fighter tries to push him through the wall.

The immovable elbow theory relates that the elbow should remain a constant one to one-and-a-half fists distance from the body to avoid the restrained bridge or "flying elbow disease" of Wing Chun. The "elbow down power" is maintained to link the hands with the body structure.

Upright structure can be viewed as a physical manifestation of the centerline and economy of motion principle. That coupled with the fact that human beings have a human structure and not a simian structure, shows that standing erect is more economical for Wing

Chun movements than leaning forward or backward, left or right. To maintain the upright structure, a practitioner raises the chest and extends the pelvis in one line. The back is always ahead of the heels. The classics tell to keep the head as if suspended from above and to allow the *hei (qi)* to sink to the *dan tian* (field of elixir). In this way a practitioner can move freely and respond in all eight directions.

Man sao (asking hand) and *wu sao* (guarding hand) are two important concepts that refer to the hands in Yip Man Wing Chun. The asking hand is the hand that asks the opponent a question. The guard hand is the hand that protects. Based on where the intention is, either hand can be an asking hand or a guard hand.

Eye sensitivity is most important at a distance, bridge sensitivity is most important at close range. The eyes are used to capture all the information needed prior to contact with an opponent. Eyes are trained to not only see but receive. The gaze is active, not fixed, and the practitioner looks to see how an opponent can be a threat to him. Practitioners often begin with the idea of looking at the elbows and knees. Intermediate students generally look at the shoulders for rising, falling, and torquing. Advanced students train to look at the opponent's chest and to be able to detect the slightest rotation or change in the depth of field. Other systems of martial arts utilize rotation to generate force. A practitioner can perceive an opponent's intended attack by recognizing change of depth of field by watching the opponent's chest. One does not look at the face, as an opponent may feint with the use of the eyes. Eyes must be trained not to blink during combat, especially with weapons. Wing Chun has a saying on the use of the eyes which relates: *"Yao ying da ying; mo ying da yieng"* (When you see form, strike form; when there is no form, strike shadow). This statement is profound, for it presumes one has mastered the unfixed gaze, and informs that a practitioner cannot always rely on the shapes and forms that are presented.

"Lui lao hui soong; lut sao jik chung" (As my opponent comes, I receive him; as he leaves, I escort him; upon loss of contact, I charge forward). Mastering this principle is the core of understanding Yip Man Wing Chun. These eight characters embody the essence of the Wing Chun practitioner during combat and *chi sao*. *Lui lao* is when an opponent comes; one stands one's ground and receives him. The feeling is relaxed, but one never gives up ones own ground. It also refers to slowing the opponent down, discontinuing his forward aggression, and guiding him elsewhere. *Hui soong* is when the opponent retreats, one escorts him and adds to his retreat. One follows the opponent with proactive perception until he makes a mistake. *Lut sao* is when the opponent or practitioner disengages or one does not have

contact with the bridges. *Jik chung* refers to the aggressive straight entry and blasting of an opponent when one does not have control of the bridges. The closest analogy is opening a flood gate or a water dam; the released water will bowl one over. We can also explain this with an analogy of meeting a friend at a train station. As he is coming, I wait to receive him. When he is going home, I escort him. If I do not make contact with him, I have to go forward to contact him.

The saying *"lien siu dai da"* (linking defense to bring in offense), is commonly poorly translated as "simultaneous block and strike." It touches on the nature of offense and defense, conceptually, in terms of energy. What this means is that when my opponent attacks, typically, I wish to intercept him, that is, striking him and defending myself at the same time. The most efficient means of this is to simply strike your opponent's strike, and kick your opponent's kick. A less efficient means is to use one hand to defend with a tool (e.g., *tan, pak, lop*) while using the other hand at the same time to strike.

"Bo lay tao, dao fu san, tiet kiu sao" (Glass head, bean-curd body, and iron bridges). Glass head and bean-curd body means that one does not want to absorb a strike, so one gets out of the way. One changes the centerline and creates a new line of entry. This is how one can overcome martial arts that emphasize power. Iron bridges refers to aligning the body in perfect structure to break into an opponent's attack and that the hands must protect the body and the head.

"Kuen yao sum faat" (Fist comes from the heart). This is one of the rich teachings of Wing Chun. It has several levels of meaning. The beginner may look at this as a clue to where the *jik chung chui* originates in the first set. It can also mean that the fist (boxing, style) comes from the heart of the practitioner. In olden days, Chinese believed that thought came from the heart. Even today, Chinese use the expression, "In my heart I think . . ." What this means is that the individual's style comes from their personality. This can also explain the variations of Yip Man Wing Chun.

"Sao lao jung sien" (The hand remains in the centerline) posits that the hand is normally placed in the center for this is the optimal position from which to strike and defend.

"Da sao jik siu sao" (The striking hand also functions simultaneously as the defending hand). Wing Chun techniques are efficient; Hence a strike is not just a strike but also can be used as a defending technique at the same time.

"Mo keung da" (Don't force your strike). Conserve energy by only striking when there is an opportunity. Otherwise, valuable energy is wasted by striking at a well-protected opponent.

"Mo luen da" (Don't waste your strikes). Don't just strike

blindly and throw out a hundred strikes; rather, always throw a decisive strike. One should take one's time and make the majority of one's strikes count.

CONCLUSION

Yip Man Wing Chun, known for its simplicity, directness, economy of motion, and encapsulation of the essential Wing Chun principles, has earned itself a place in martial arts history due to its mass popularity. Yip Man Wing Chun can be summarized with the oral tradition, *"Sao gerk seung siu, mo jit jiu"* (Hands and feet defend accordingly, there are no secret unstoppable maneuvers). It is a practical, no-nonsense system evolving with the current times. With over one million practitioners around the world, Grandmaster Yip Man's legacy lives on.

CHAPTER 2

YUEN KAY-SAN WING CHUN KUEN

Calm and intelligent, powerful and dynamic, the Yuen Kay-San style is one of the major sects of Wing Chun kuen. Centered in the city of Guangzhou and lead by Grandmaster Sum Nung, Yuen Kay-San Wing Chun kuen is renowned for its simplicity, directness, and devastating efficacy.

HISTORY AND DEVELOPMENT

The true founders of Wing Chun kuen remain lost in the mists of time and shrouded in the veils of legend. Beyond the legends, it is known that the mid-nineteenth century masters of Wing Chun were members of the Hung Suen Hay Ban (Red Junk Opera Company). Among them were performers Wong Wah-Bo, Leung Yee-Tai, Gao Lo Chung (Tall Man Chung), and the ancestor of the Yuen Kay-San style, Dai Fa Min Kam (Painted Face Kam).

Yuen Kay-San was born in 1889 to a wealthy merchant father who operated the fireworks store on Chen Bak Road in Foshan, Guangdong. The fifth child of his family, he was often called Yuen Lo-Jia (Yuen "The Fifth"). When Yuen Kay-San was still quite young, his father engaged a student of Dai Fa Min Kam's named Fok Bo-Chuen to teach him the skills of Wing Chun kuen.

Fok Bo-Chuen worked as a constable in Foshan and his knowledge of the martial arts was remarkable. In addition to his training under Dai Fa Min Kam, he also received lessons from Wong Wah-Bo. Yuen Kay-San studied under Fok intensely for many years. He eventually became highly accomplished in boxing, the practice dummies, the pole, the knives, the flying darts, the iron sand palm, and other skills. Studying alongside Yuen Kay-San was his elder brother, Yuen Chai-Wan, known by the nickname Dao Po Chai (Pock Face Chai).

Although Yuen Kay-San had developed profound ability under the guidance of Fok Bo-Chuen, he was still eager for more knowledge. Thus, he approached the famed and feared Fung Siu-Ching, seeking further instruction.

Fung Siu-Ching was a Shunde native who learned Wing Chun from Dai Fa Min Kam in Guangzhou where he worked as a military marshal. During the end of the Qing dynasty, Fung was also rumored to have served as a guard for the Sichuan governor. His profession required him to use his Wing Chun skills in real combat on a daily basis, often in life or death situations. This led him to develop phenomenal skills and a profound depth of fighting experience.

When Yuen Kay-San came to him, Fung Siu-Ching was already quite old and was just about to retire. Although initially hesitant, Yuen's dedication won him over, and Fung decided to delay his retirement and accept Yuen as his disciple. Moving to Foshan, Fung spent his remaining few years at the Yuen Family Estate in Mulberry Gardens. Studying alongside Yuen Kay-San at this time were Yuen Chai-Wan, Ma Jung-Yiu (the son of Ma Bok-Leung), Lo Hao-Po of the Ying Joy teahouse, Au Shi of the Fai Jee Street butcher shop, Leung Yan, and others. In Foshan, Fung Siu-Ching polished and refined the Wing Chun application skills and extreme close range fighting techniques of Yuen Kay-San to a very high level. Yuen Kay-San followed Fung Siu-Ching until the old marshal passed away at the age of seventy-three.

Yuen Kay–San Jong Si, founder of the system.

Throughout his lessons, Yuen Kay-San had always paid close attention and taken detailed notes, becoming one of the first to systematically record Wing Chun's concepts and principles. When his training was complete, he spent his time analyzing the scientific principles of Wing Chun kuen. Combining together and refining all the knowledge he had acquired, he developed a profound understanding of Wing Chun kuen and reached an extremely advanced level of skill.

Yuen Kay-San was quite wealthy and aside from his part time work as a lawyer for the government of Foshan he did little with his time but practice Wing Chun kuen. Even though he was fairly well known in the area, he always kept his knowledge of martial arts quiet, never opening a school and always doing his best to avoid publicity and confrontation. He believed that his abilities should only be used to defend himself and for practice. When forced to use his knowledge for self-defense, Yuen Kay-San took the contests as learning experiences. Many of his victories, in both boxing and weapons fighting, became the subject of local newspaper articles and stories written by journalists such as Au Sui-Jee in the 1930s and more recently by his grandson, Yuen Jo-Tong.

Dr. Sum Nung, Grandmaster of Yuen Kay-San Wing Chun kuen. Guangzhou, late 1960s.

Over the years, Yuen Kay-San would sometimes drop by Tien Hoi, a local restaurant, to take tea. At the restaurant worked a good friend of his named Cheung Bo. Cheung Bo, a chef by trade, was a large and powerful man who taught Wing Chun kuen's "separate techniques" to a small group of fellow staff members at night when the establishment was closed. Cheung Bo had a great reputation as a fighter and was rumored to have learned the art from Wan Yuk-Sang, a Nationalist Army doctor said to have been the student of Au Shi.

One of Cheung Bo's students at the time was a hard working young boy named Sum Nung. Born in South America in 1926, Sum Nung moved to China with relatives as a child. Settling in Foshan, Sum Nung eventually took a job at the restaurant where Cheung Bo worked in order to help support his family during the difficult times preceding World War II. Even though quite young, Sum Nung was very interested in the martial arts and in the late 1930s he began training in Wing Chun kuen under Cheung Bo's guidance. Although the style was simple, it built in him a very solid foundation. At the same time, Sum Nung began his medical training under Wan Yuk-Sang.

After dining at Tien Hoi, Yuen Kay-San would sometimes remain behind to watch the staff practice their Wing Chun kuen. While observing, he would stay quiet and would never comment nor criticize. Over time, however, he grew to admire the dedication of

Sum Nung and eventually asked Cheung Bo if he could take over the young boy's instruction. Cheung Bo, knowing and respecting the tremendous quality of Yuen Kay-San's Wing Chun kuen, and realizing he had already taught Sum Nung as much as he could, happily agreed and soon introduced Sum Nung to Yuen Kay-San.

Sum Nung was hesitant at first. He had been learning from Cheung Bo for a few years and saw the elderly and slender Yuen Kay-San as a stark contrast to his young and powerful teacher. Touching arms at Yuen's invitation, however, Sum found that he could move only once or twice before Yuen cut him off and left him unable to continue. Following this quick but profound demonstration of Yuen Kay-San's skills, Sum Nung soon became his treasured disciple.

Over the years, Yuen Kay-San and Sum Nung spent much time together, constantly practicing Wing Chun kuen. When not practicing, Sum would spend time sitting with Yuen and would listen as his teacher spoke of Wing Chun's concepts.

As a young adult in the 1940s, Sum Nung traveled to the nearby city of Guangzhou, introducing the teachings of Yuen Kay-San to the region. In order to support himself before his medical practice was established, he taught Wing Chun kuen and provided medical services to members of local Trade Unions such as the Restaurant Workers Union and the Iron Workers Union. Although Sum Nung, like Yuen Kay-San before him, did not boast of his abilities nor seek out conflict, he did on occasion have friendly tests of skill with practitioners of other martial art styles. Though he did not often talk of these encounters out of respect for his opponents, it is said he never met with defeat and developed an unsurpassed reputation in the area for the quality of his Wing Chun.

Grandmaster Sum Nung and some students in Guangzhou in the late 1960s (from left to right) Ngo Lui-Kay, Dr. Sum Nung, Leung Dai-Chiu, and Dong Chuen-Kam.

In the mid 1950s, when Yuen Kay-San fell ill, he told Sum Nung that he was afraid that after he died, his name and contributions to Wing Chun would be forgotten. Thus, when Yuen Kay-San passed away in 1956, Sum Nung named his style Yuen Kay-San Wing Chun kuen, in honor and memory of his teacher.

Returning to Guangzhou, Sum Nung began working in a local clinic. Due to the changing conditions following the rise to power of the communists and the subsequent Cultural Revolution, Dr. Sum Nung taught Wing Chun privately and quietly, not wanting to attract attention.

Over the years, accepting only those he felt were upright and trustworthy, Grandmaster Sum Nung has gone on to train a generation of outstanding pupils. Among Sum Nung's students (with apologies, far to many to list here) are Sum Jee (his uncle, who was previously a very good practitioner of Hung ga kuen), Kwok Jin-Fun, Leung Gwing-Chiu (now in the United States), Dong Chuen-Kam (deceased), Ngo Lui-Kay (Ao Leiqi, now in Canada), Kwok Wan-Ping (who brought the art to Hong Kong in the late 1960s), and Lee Chi-Yiu (in Hong Kong). Other students, such as Teddy Wong who moved to New York, and Tom Wong, who relocated to Los Angeles, helped introduced the style to the United States. Several of Kwok Wan-Ping's disciples also moved to North America, including Tse Chung-Fei (British Columbia), Chow Kwok-Tai (Toronto), and Lee Chung-Ming (Washington D.C.).

Ngo Lui–Kay (Ao Leiqi) Sifu uses an application from the *Sup Yee Sik's Bak Hok Kum Wu.*

BASIC MOVEMENTS

The movements of Yuen Kay-San Wing Chun kuen are a blend of the linear and circular, internal and external, which greatly enhances the versatility and effectiveness of the style. The lines and circles, the hard and soft, are used in combination in the form and in the application of the movements. They are relaxed and flexible, yet they express explosive and elastic energies that grant them considerable power while retaining maximum control and adaptability.

Stances include the *yee jee kim yeung ma* ("*yee*" character clamping groin horse), which is the fundamental posture of the style. Its structure includes the toes facing inwards and grabbing the floor, the knees pressing to one-fist distance, the buttocks tucked under, the body leaning neither forward nor back, the stomach and chest held in, the shoulders relaxed, the elbows closed on the center line, and the head suspended. *Pien ma* (side horse) turns the body as a connected unit, emptying the vast majority of weight onto one leg while maintaining many of the structural points of the *kim yeung ma*. *Jin ma* (arrow horse) uses a configuration similar to pien ma, but for stepping rather then turning. *Yee ma* (moving horse) increases one's mobility with linear, angular, or circular steps.

Ngo Lui–Kay Sifu performs a movement from the *muk yan jong*.

Complementing these are postures such as the kneeling side horse, slant horse, and additional, specialized stances, all of which can be used as powerful offensive and defensive tactics. One of the greatest strengths of these postures lies in their ability to be combined in almost any conceivable manner, turning simple stances into a surprisingly flexible footwork system.

Hand weapons are comprised of the pounding *chung chui* (thrusting punch), the whipping *gwa chui* (hanging punch; backfist strike), and a few other configurations. Enhancing the fists are many different techniques that strike with the palm, palm edge, wrist, finger and thumb tips, etc. Although primarily offensive weapons, even these simple techniques contain defensive aspects such as structures which cut-off and check an opponent's actions.

Leg methods are composed of *chuen sum gerk* (heart piercing kick), *wang ding gerk* (side nailing kick), *fu mei gerk* (tiger tail kick), and *liu yum gerk* (lifting yin kick), among others. While the leg techniques appear simple on the surface, each is a compound motion containing many principles and offering many possibilities. Beginning motions often include evasions, intermediary movements usually contain interceptions and disruptions, and the actual strikes themselves can sometimes be broken down into several distinct kicking techniques.

Although the hands and feet are powerful weapons, Yuen Kay-San Wing Chun kuen also employs methods of striking with the head, shoulders, elbows, hips, knees, and most of the parts in-between. Accompanying its famed striking methods, techniques for uprooting, controlling, choking, joint locking, counter joint-locking, sweeping, and other tactics are also contained in both the separate techniques and the forms.

FORMS AND TRAINING

Yuen Kay-San Wing Chun is composed of the *sup yee sik* (twelve forms), the *kuen* (fist forms), the *muk yan jong* (wooden dummy), the *sun hei gwai yuen* (kidney breathing return invigoration), the *luk dim boon gwun* (six-and-a-half-point pole), the *yee jee seung dao* (*"yee"* character double knives), and other skills. In these are contained the movements and concepts of the style.

Rene Ritchie applies a joint locking technique from the *muk yan jong's* butterfly palms section.

The *sup yee sik* (twelve forms) descend from the separate techniques taught by Cheung Bo. They are compact in structure yet contain many of the elements essential to a good Wing Chun foundation and are ideal for early training. Although perhaps not as refined as the techniques of Yuen Kay-San Wing Chun proper, these same attributes make them quite valuable as a sort of crash-course in Wing Chun self-defense for those who require simple skill yet do not have the time or desire to delve more deeply into the art. The *sup yee sik* are composed of twelve main sets and several extensions. Due to Cheung Bo's size, it was said that he did not keep his elbows on the centerline but rather used a more open arm

Ngo Lui–Kay Sifu trains the barring pole from the *luk dim boon gwun* movements.

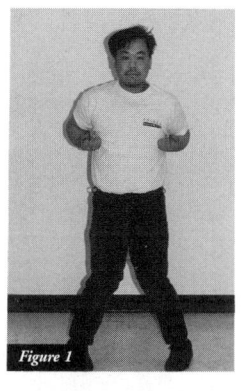

Wilson Woo demonstrates single dragon punch movements from the *Sup Yee Sik*. (Fig. 1) Beginning in *yee jee kim yeung ma*; (Fig. 2) punching to the side; (Fig. 3) turning and alternating punches; (Figs. 4, 5) *lien wan chui*; (Fig. 6) turning with a *bong sao*; (Fig. 7) punching in the new direction.

structure, compensating with rapid stance changes. Some of the *sup yee sik* retain Cheung Bo's characteristic wide-arm *kao sao* (capturing arms) and quick defensive stance changes.

Amongst the twelve forms are *jee ng chui* (meridian punch), the fundamental drill practiced in the *yee jee kim yeung ma*. *Jee ng chui* uses the *chung chui* which shoots along the body's central line. Its extensions include *sam sing chui* (three star punch) and, the rapid-fire *lien wan chui* (linked chain punch). Similar sets include *pien chui* (side punch) which develops the connection with turning, *duk lung chui* (single dragon punch) which further trains the turning and introduces motions like *bong sao* (wing arm), and *jin chui* (arrow punch) which adds stepping to the structure. These basic techniques help the practitioner "combine the power of the stance, waist, and arms" (Figs. 1–7).

The *sup yee sik* also include hand sets such as *loi lim yum yeung jeung* (inside/outside yin and yang palms), which combines the *tan sao* (dispersing arm) and the folding *fook sao* (controlling arm) into a form densely packed with techniques and principles. Other such sets include *ngoi dap* (inside join) which cycles an inside controlling technique with an outside *huen sao* (circling arm) and its extension *ngoi lop* (inside grasp) and their opposites, *ngoi dap* (outside join), and *ngoi lop* (outside grasp).

In addition, there are compound movements like *pok yic jeung* (flapping wing palm) and combinations such as *bak hok kum wu* (white crane catches the fox), a punishing technique which melds a *saat kiu* (killing bridge) with a *gwok ma* (angle horse) take down.

The fist forms of Yuen Kay-San Wing Chun are *siu lien tao, chum kiu,* and *biu jee.* Although movements are executed consecutively in the forms, they are not choreographed battles against imaginary opponents. When practicing, attention is focused on each individual motion. Actual techniques and concepts are separate and distinct. They are collected in the forms, encyclopedia-like, to be applied as the practitioner requires-when, where, and how they are needed. *Siu lien tao* develops the foundation, while *chum kiu* and *biu jee* train "the long to short and short to long." Although at first glance, *chum kiu* may appear to contain predominantly defensive bridging movements while *biu jee* may seem to consist of more aggressive, offensive movements, in Wing Chun the barriers between offense and defense blur and motions can easily assume the characteristics of either depending on the circumstances.

Siu lien tao (little first training), the essential set, is practiced completely in the *yee jee kim yeung ma* stance. It contains numerous seed techniques and concepts like the *sup jee sao* (*"sup"* character arm), *tan sao, fook sao, wu sao* (protecting arm), *pai jang* (hacking elbows), *tun sao* (swallowing arm), *por jung sao* (center cleaving arm), *bong sao,* and the characteristic outward *lop sao* (grasping arm) which ends almost every section. *Siu lien tao* is often considered the archival set of Wing Chun, conveying the essence of the system in an incredibly refined, yet deeply profound manner (Figs. 8–18).

Chum kiu (sinking bridge), the second form, integrates motions with *pien ma* turning and *jin ma* stepping. It also introduces kicking techniques such as *chuen sum gerk* and *wang ding gerk,* along with several different types of *bong sao* performed at high, middle, and low levels, a version of the *lan sao* (barring arm), *kao geng sao* (neck detaining arm), and other techniques (Figs. 19–27).

Biu jee (darting fingers), the third and final fist form, develops more advanced tactics. Although a relatively stationary form, it does

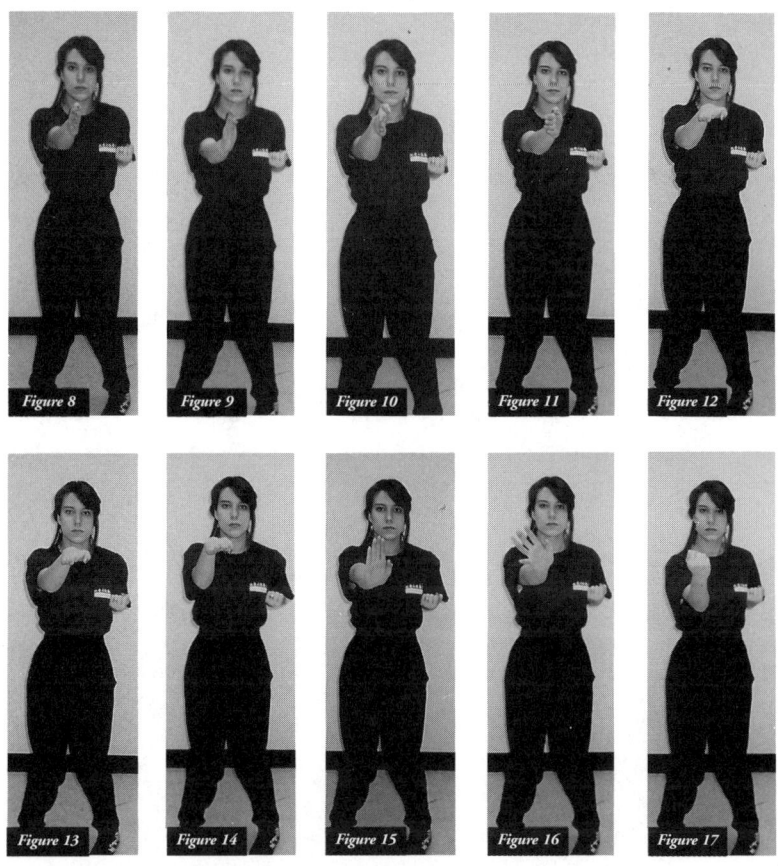

Georgia Dow performs the *sup jee sao* from the beginning of *siu lien tao*. Opening the hand following a meridian punch (Fig. 8). Moving the wrist down, up, in, and out (Figs. 9–12). Turning the wrist and moving it in and out (Figs. 13, 14). (Fig. 15) Pushing the palm forward. Grasping hand (Fig. 16). Commencing withdrawal (Fig. 17).

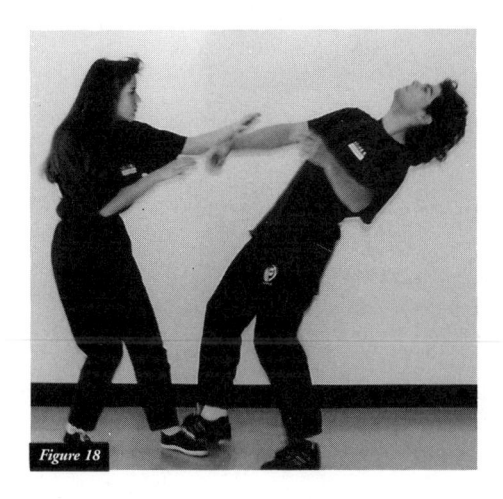

Georgia applies a shoveling over bridge from *siu lien tao* to slice into her opponent.

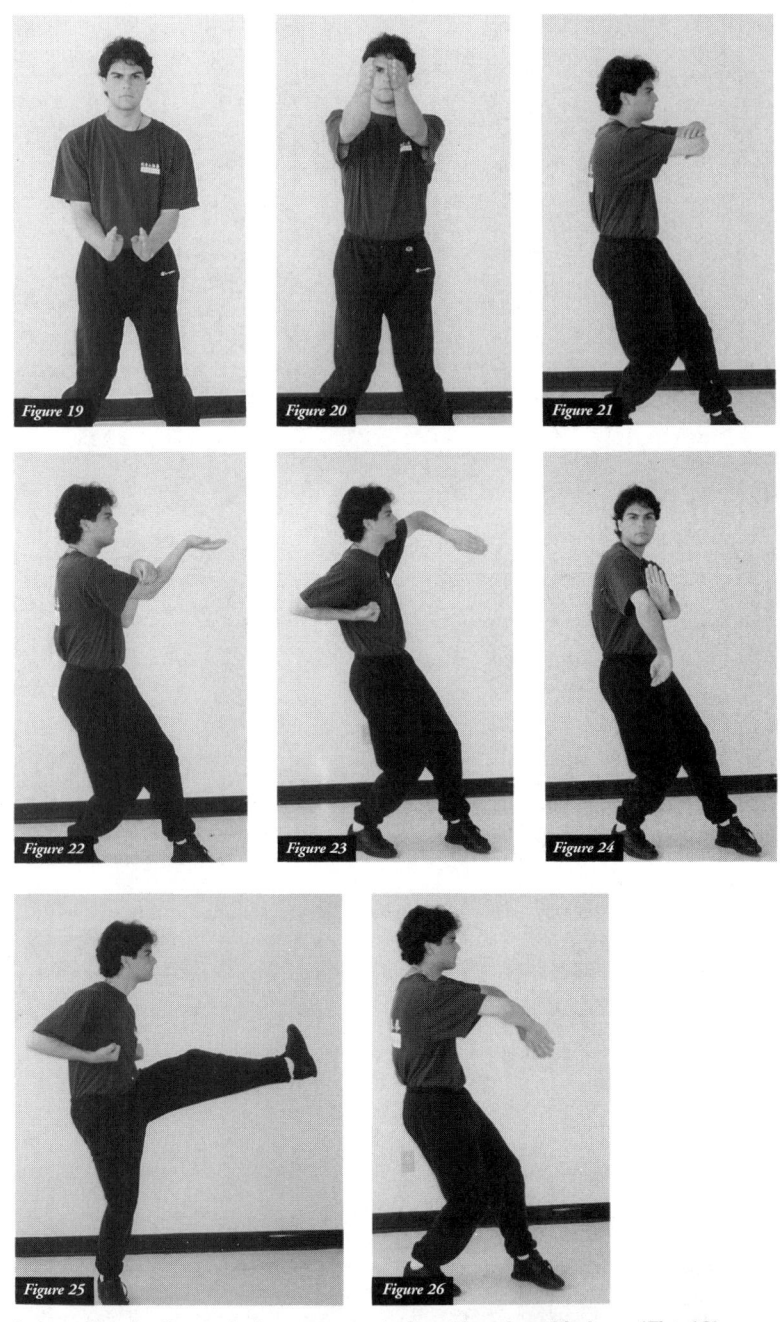

Antony Casella demonstrates movements from the *chum kiu* form. (Fig. 19) Sinking the bridges. (Fig. 20) Darting the fingers. (Fig. 21) Barring with the arm and hacking with the elbow. (Fig. 22) Detaining with the wrist and butting with the palm. (Fig. 23) High wing arm. (Fig. 24) low wing arm and protecting arm. (Fig. 25) Heart piercing kick. (Fig. 26) Throwing wings.

Figure 27

Antony applies a choke from the movement following the throwing wings in chum kiu.

contain such footwork as *yee ma* and sequences including *kup jang* (covering elbows), *gang sao* (crossing arms), *saat kiu,* and *gao san* (saving body) (Figs. 28–30).

Muk yan jong (wooden dummy) is the most famous of the Yuen Kay-San Wing Chun training aids. The wooden dummy is constructed to match the size of its intended user and is composed of a main body post, two high-level arms, a single mid-level arm, and a low-level leg. When originally developed, the dummy was buried quite deeply in the ground and surrounded by loose earth. As apartments grew more common, this arrangement became impractical, if not impossible (especially if one lived above ground level), so many have since redesigned the wooden dummy to include a supporting base. The movements of the wooden dummy form help to develop the bridges and body structure, build precision and accuracy in movements, and aid in the development of short-range, explosive energy.

The form itself contains movements from the twelve techniques, the three forms, and introduces motions such as *wu dip jeung* (butterfly palms), *poon tan bong* (half-dispersing, half-wing), and *hay sup* (rising knee). The form is also practiced as *hong jong* (air dummy). This is simply the dummy techniques practiced on their own, without the actual physical dummy construct. In addition to the *muk yan jong,* other training aids include the rattan circle, chopstick work, candle hitting, and sandbag striking.

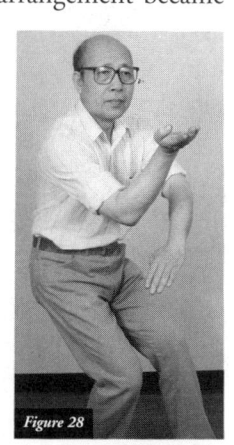

Figure 28

From *Biu Jee*, Ngo Lui–Kay Sifu assumes the crossing arms.

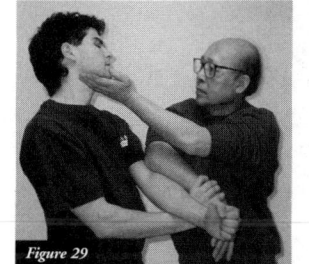

Figure 29

Ngo Lui–Kay Sifu applies the covering elbow and throat strike to counter a grab.

The *sun hei gwai yuen* (kidney breathing invigoration) are short *hei gung* (*qigong*) like sets typically practiced after training to re-energize and revitalize the body. They were said to have been taught to the Wing Chun followers by a monk who, while observing their practice, admired the quality of their fighting skills and so passed along the *sun hei gwai yuen* in order to improve their health. The *sun hei gwai yuen* include exercises like *shun hei* (yielding breath) and *gong hung* (expanding chest) (Figs. 31–34).

The *luk dim boon gwun* (six-and-a-half-point pole) represents the long-range weapons training of Yuen Kay-San Wing Chun kuen. The long pole is a single headed weapon and is never spun or twirled. It uses techniques that require the practitioner to send power through the wood, out the striking point, and into the target. In addition to the standard structure, pole training incorporates stances like the *sei ping ma* (quadrilateral level horse) and *ding jee ma* ("T" stance). Pole techniques include six-and-a-half simple "points" (techniques/concepts) like *siu chum gwun* (dispelling pole), *cheung gwun* (spearing pole), and several extrapolations such as *taan gwun* (side to side pole) that cover all basic angles for both offense and defense. These are trained in form, using training devices such as balls suspended on string, small objects scattered on the floor, etc. and later with partners in drills, both structured and free-style.

The *yee jee seung dao* (double knives) comprise the short-range weapon aspect of the style. In contrast to the pole, they favor methods and motions almost identical to the fists and can

Figure 30

Ngo Lui–Kay Sifu demonstrates a moving stance take down.

Figure 31 *Figure 32* *Figure 33* *Figure 34*

Rene Ritchie exercises movements from *sun hei gwai yuen's* expanding chest set. (Fig. 31) Opening. (Fig. 32) Expanding out. (Fig. 33) Expanding up. (Fig. 34).

be seen to act as extensions of the hands. The Yuen Kay-San knives always have the blades extended out towards the opponent, and are never folded backwards across the forearm. When applied, the Wing Chun knives cut the first available target and progress from there to finish the opponent. With the fundamental drill of *gang dao* (crossing knives), a practitioner learns to wield, control, and change the two knives economically and efficiently while stationary and while moving in all directions. Subsequent motions introduce slicing, stabbing, and a variety of other simple, elegant, yet frighteningly effective techniques (Figs. 35–37).

Figure 35

A technique from the *Yee Jee Seung Dao* is practiced by Ngo Lui–Kay Sifu.

Sensitivity training and emphasis on practical application are the central theme of Yuen Kay-San Wing Chun. Starting with simple exercises and applications from fundamental movements, training progresses through a wide range of two-person drills that develop the many levels of application, from the obvious to the subtle.

San sao (separate hands) allows the numerous movements and concepts to be broken down and practiced independently. beginning with simple techniques like *lan sao chung chui* (barring arm, thrusting punch), and *gang sao gwa chui* (crossing arm, hanging punch), these exercises help develop the reflexes needed to engage forces which begin at a distance and where there is no initial contact (Figs. 38–40).

Figure 36

Figure 37

(Fig. 36) When utilizing the Knives, a practitioner usually attacks the first available target (such as the hands) and then (Fig. 37) follows up as necessary.

Chi sao (sticking arms) consists of several different drills. *Kwai bong* cycles the *bong sao, lop sao, kao sao,* and *gwa chui. Seung huen sao* (double circling arms)

Antony Casella and David Johnson drill basic *san sao*. (Fig. 38) Antony is relaxed in his *jong* (ready position) while David assumes an aggressive stance. **(Fig. 39)** David initiates a high swing that Antony counters with a barring arm and thrusting punch. **(Fig. 40)** David then follows up with a low swing, and Antony cancels it with a crossing arm while striking with a hanging punch.

Ngo Lui-Kay Sifu trains sensitivity with some of his students. (Fig. 41) Wing arm cycle. **(Fig. 42)** Circling arms. **(Fig. 43)** Rolling arms.

begins with simple circling motions but later adds basic attacks and defenses. *Luk sao* (rolling arms) starts with a *tan-*, *fook-*, and *bong*-based platform and forms the basis for the *chi sao* exercise proper. It is said "sticking arms is like asking the way." This can be interpreted to mean that through *chi sao*, the opponent's actions inform the practitioner how best to overcome them. Thus, in a way, the opponent causes his or her own defeat (Figs. 41–43).

These forms of training serve to bridge the gap between practice and actual combat. As with other types of training, the initial exercises are simple and predictable, with more subtle, instinctive, and skillful changes being introduced as feeling increases. This deconstruction and exploration helps to release the practitioners from pattern and repetition and allows them to apply their knowledge creatively and spontaneously, discovering the almost limitless potentials which come from the seemingly simple looking movements.

CONCEPTS AND PRINCIPLES

Yuen Kay-San Wing Chun kuen contains many concepts and principles such as linked attack and defense, economy of motion, reflexive response and adaptation according to conditions. In addition, several formal sets have been handed down through the generations. These sets include the *sup yee faat* (twelve methods), the *faat moon* (methodology), the *yiu ku* (important rhymed formulae), the *yiu jee* (important ideas), and others.

The *sup yee faat* (twelve methods), while simple on the surface can provide a gateway to deeper understanding of the style. They are contained in the single character words *dap* (join), *jeet* (intercept), *chum* (sink), *biu* (dart), *chi* (stick), *mo* (touch), *tong* (press), *dong* (swing), *tun* (swallow), *chit* (slice), *tao* (steal), and *lao* (leak). Some also include *kao* (detain) and *saat* (kill) in their listings.

Other basic drills include waist pulling, demonstrated by Deon Weir, with a hanging punch.

The *faat moon* (methodology) and similar writings such as the *yiu ku* (important rhymed formulae), consist almost entirely of four character poetic couplets. These couplets embody tactical advice on the use of Yuen Kay-San Wing Chun kuen. Among the *faat moon* are:

- *Lui lao hui soong* (Receive what comes, accompany what leaves).
- *Fung lut jik jong* (Charge straight when free).
- *Yee yao jai gong* (Use soft to overcome hard).
- *Gong yao ping yung* (Hard and soft combine in use).

Ngo Lui–Kay Sifu uses throat lock to counter a thrusting punch attack.

- *Yee ching jai dong* (Use stillness to overcome movement).
- *Yee yat toy lo* (Use rest to overcome fatigue).

Yiu jee (important ideas) and similar writings are expressed in sets of five character poetic couplets. In general, they seek to provide insight on how the Yuen Kay-San Wing Chun practitioners can train to develop their skills based on working hard, being healthy, studying diligently, being nimble, using the eyes, being first, being viscous, and being fast. The *yiu jee* include:

- *Fa chuk dui sao chi* (Explore changes by sticking with a partner).
- *Dui gang yiu jong tao* (Use a mirror and dummy to aid in this pursuit).
- *Lik chui jee gok chuen* (Strength is aware, it follows and changes with feeling).
- *Lien juk bat ting lao* (Continue without stopping or staying).

CONCLUSION

As a result of the tireless efforts of Grandmaster Sum Nung and his many students and descendants, Yuen Kay-San Wing Chun kuen has remained alive and thriving in China and has spread to Hong Kong, Canada, the United States, Australia, and other places. Today, it remains a vibrant and important part of the past and future of the Wing Chun kuen family of styles.

CHAPTER 3

Gu Lao Wing Chun Kuen

When Leung Jan retired from his pharmacy in Foshan he returned to his native Gu Lao village. There, the renowned doctor passed along a simple yet remarkably profound style of Wing Chun, the *sei sup dim* (forty points) system.

HISTORY AND DEVELOPMENT

Legends say that during the Qing dynasty, Yim Wing-Chun and her husband, Leung Bok-Chao, taught the second generation practitioners of Wing Chun kuen. These students worked as a Red Boat Opera troupe by day and anti-Qing revolutionaries by night.

This generation of students included Wong Wah-Bo, Leung Yee-Tai, Dai Fa Min Kam, Gao Lo Chung, Hung Gun Biu, and Leung Lan-Kwai. Many of the opera members had training in Siu Lam fist and pole techniques, acrobatics, and various two man sets. They were master choreographers, performing every night the opera was in a town. The Red Boat members were also affiliated with many anti-Qing groups including the Tien Dei Wui (Heaven and Earth Society) and their goal was to overthrow the Manchurians and restore the Ming to the throne of China. Wing Chun kuen was their art of choice. As an opera troupe, they could move about freely at any time without question. They could hide knives in their loose fitting garments and assassinate Qing officials in the narrow alleys of southern China.

Yim Wing-Chun's art was composed of simple, direct, economical movements and was conceptual in content. Training consisted of some forty or so repetitive techniques that could be practiced in the air, with a partner, on a wooden dummy, or with knives. At this point in the development of Wing Chun kuen, there were no structured forms as it was the goal of this training to be immediately applied to serve the purpose of self-defense or assassination.

Eventually, Wong Wah-Bo and Leung Yee-Tai took on a student named Leung Jan. Leung studied the loose techniques and the art in the forms that were choreographed by the opera members. Leung became known for his application of Wing Chun in *gong sao* (talking hands—a fight) and became known as the King of Wing Chun, or the Gong Sao Wong (Talking Hands King). Leung Jan has also become the famous subject of books like Au Sui-Jee's 1930s work *Foshan Jan Sin-Sang* (Mr. Jan of Foshan) and today, the subject of movies.

While much of Wing Chun's early history remains unclear, it is known that Leung Jan, a native of Gu Lao village, became an herbalist and opened an herb shop on Fai Jee Street in the nearby city of Foshan. The shop was called Jan Sang Tong (Mr. Jan's Hall). There, Leung Jan went on to teach his sons Leung Bik and Leung Chun, and a few, select students like Chan Wah-Shun, Muk Yan Wah (Wooden Man Wah), Chu Yuk Kwai (Butcher Kwai), and Fung Wah.

Robert Chu (Chu Sau–Lei) Sifu performs *siu fook fu*, one of the forty points passed along by Leung Jan in Gu Lao village.

Upon reaching retirement age, Leung Jan returned to his native village of Gu Lao. While there, he taught a few local students his synthesis of Wing Chun. Instead of focusing on teaching the Wing Chun forms, dummy, and weapons sets, he centered his training on forty short drills, pole techniques, and double knife techniques. These became known as the Gu Lao *sei sup dim* (Gu Lao's forty points) Wing Chun system.

***Hok bong*, one of the points that may reflect the crane influence in Wing Chun.**

The forty points were the loose expression and application of Wing Chun kuen. They were not inseparable or different from the other forms of Wing Chun. Leung Jan simply chose to pass on the art in its separate form when he retired to Gu Lao.

Among those who learned the forty points system was Leung Jan's grand-student, Tam Yeung. In Gu Lao, when Tam Yeung was a student, it would cost a small fortune to learn even one point. Co-author Robert Chu came to learn this system from his good friend and sifu, Kwan Jong-Yuen, who in turn learned the art from Tam Yeung.

BASIC MOVEMENTS

The forty points include classical and metaphorical names for each of the movements, which may indicate a Siu Lam origin of some of the techniques. Most of these names have been replaced using modern jargon. Although few in number and perhaps not as intricate as the classical forms of Wing Chun, the forty points serve to review the Wing Chun system for the advanced practitioner, and function as an excellent teaching tool for beginning students. They are trained in a repetitive manner, alternating left and right sides.

Biu jee point.

One should not simply look at the forty points as techniques, but as tactics to teach the fighting skills of Wing Chun. When the basics are mastered, a student can then do combinations and permutations of the techniques while moving left and right, with high and low stances, at high, middle, or low levels, to the front and back, and/or while advancing or adjusting the steps. Advanced practitioners can reach the level of being able to change and vary their movements with empty-hands or the double knives.

FORMS AND TRAINING

Gu Lao Wing Chun's basics are trained through the forty points outlined below.

Gwai ma chui.

Baat gwa lung na in form and in application.

Jee ng chui (meridian punch), also known as *yat jee chung chui* (thrusting punch), is Wing Chun's signature punch. With short explosive power and a vertical fist, it is held relaxed until impact and force is exerted with the entire body.

Duen kiu (short bridge) is equivalent to the *seung chum sao* (double sinking hands) movements. In application, it teaches the concept of *por jung* (breaking the centerline). The hands are open and relaxed and cut down vertically into the opponent's attacking bridge.

Baat gwa lung na (eight directional dragon grab) uses the double *lop sao* (grabbing hands). The lead hand is held upwards in a clawing motion, while the rear hand simultaneously grabs and pulls the opponent's bridges, setting up for a kick, throw, or strike (Figs. 1, 2).

Sei mun (four gates) uses the *bai jong* (on guard stance) to exercise the left and right positions of the *jee ng ma* (forward stance) and the left and right *chum kiu ma* (bridge seeking horse) positions.

Siu fook fu (small subduing the tiger) employs an alternating left and right *gaun sao* (cultivating hand) with *fong ngan chui* (phoenix-eye fists).

Dai fook fu (big subduing the tiger) is basically the same as the *siu fook fu* but uses triangle steps to enter at an opponent's side gates.

Pien san chui (slant body punch) is the *jee ng chui* using the wing chun shift. In application one may strike to an opponent's outside gate, crossing over his attempted blow.

Biu jee (darting fingers) implies the fingers. However, in application the technique utilizes the forearm when striking the opponent.

Wan wun yiu tiet ban kiu (emergency bend at the waist and iron bridge) trains the practitioner to bend forward or backwards at will and can be coupled with hand techniques. It is similar in application to the fade and slip of western boxing.

Chum kiu (sinking bridges) is a double arm position that breaks into the centerline of the opponent.

Gwai ma chui (kneeling horse strike) utilizes the kneeling horse and a phoenix-eye fist to deliver a blow aimed at the groin. This gives an insight into Wing Chun applied at a low-line level.

Pien san jeung (slant body palm) uses the side palm as a slashing maneuver coupled with front and back shifting.

Gao dai jeung (high and low palms) are actually horizontal butterfly palms with hands facing in opposite directions.

Lien wan fai jeung (linked fast palms) utilizes a *tan sao/pak sao* (spread-open hand/slapping hand) combination followed with a circular *saat jeung/chang jeung* (killing palm/shovel palm) combination (Figs. 3–6).

Hok bong (crane wing) employs the arm in an upward ninety or forty-five degree maneuver to attack or defend.

Dai bong (big wing) is a low *bong sao* position used to defend against a low attack.

Jung bong (middle-level wing hand) is the standard middle-level *bong sao*.

Noi lim sao (inside sickle hand), the inner line hand, utilizes the *fook sao* (subduing hand) in a circular fashion (Figs. 7–9).

Ngoi lim sao (outside sickle hand), the outer line hand position, employs *tan sao* in an outward circular fashion.

Fu mei (tiger's tail) is a short backward hammer-fist strike to the opponent's groin.

Figure 3

Figure 4

Figure 5

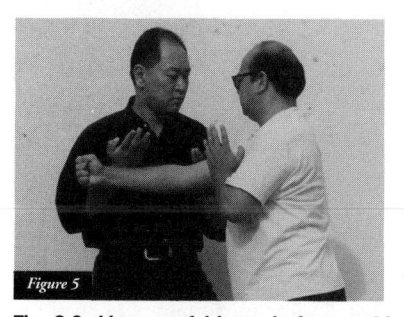

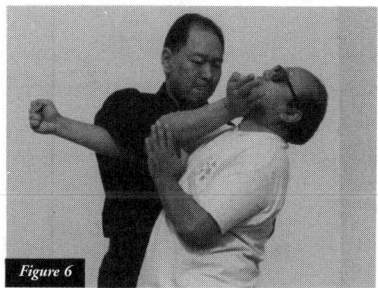

Figure 6

Fig. 3-6. *Lien wan fai jeung* **in form and in application.**

Robert Chu sifu utilizes (Fig. 7–8) the *fook sao* **in** *noi lim sao* **and (Fig. 9)** *the tan sao* **in** *ngoi lim sao.*

Gwa lung jeung (hanging dragon palm) combines the dragon claw and *jee ng chui* in combination similar to a *fook da* (subdue and hit) or *lop da* (grab and hit).

Fu biu chui (darting tiger blow) is the equivalent of *fook sao* combined with a phoenix-eye fist strike.

Sam jin chui (three arrow blows), done singly (high, middle, and low), or with both hands alternating straight punches similar to *lien wan chui* (linked punches).

Sam bai fut (three bows to Buddha) utilizes the *tan sao, pak sao,* and *gum sao* (pinning hand) to stop multiple blows.

Dip jeung (butterfly palm) is comparable to the *bo pai jeung* (shield holding palm) attack and defense.

Siu poon sao (small rolling hands) trains the rolling hands of Wing Chun.

Poon sao (rolling hand) is similar to a close body *pak sao/lao sao* (slapping hand/slipping hand) combination. It is the primary transitional move in Wing Chun.

Juk da (slanting strike) is equivalent to the slant body *jut da* (choke and hit).

Dip jeung.

Juk kiu (slanting bridge) is essentially *tan da* (spread-open and hit) done with a shift.

Ding jeung (hammer palms) are comparable to the second section of *siu lien tao* utilizing the *gum sao*. There are four positions: left, right, double front, and double rear.

Ping lan sao (level obstruction hand) is the equivalent of the *kwun sao* (rolling arm) or *tan/bong* position.

Loi kiu (double bridges) utilize a double *tan sao* position to bridge the gap on an opponent.

Chung jeung (thrusting palm) is the forward palm strike of Wing Chun done to the opponent's face or chest.

Fan cup chui (flipping upper cut) is similar to the *chao chui* (bouncing punch) from the *chum kiu* set.

Cup da sao (covering hitting hand) utilizes the *bong sao* immediately followed up with a *lop sao* and *gwa chui* (downward back fist).

Seung lung (double dragons) are the double straight punches.

Pien san dip jeung (side body butterfly palm) are alternating low palm strikes.

Ping lan sao.

Charp chui (piercing strike) is basically a *wu sao* (protecting hand) performed with a fist and combined with a straight punch.

Bik bong (pressing wing) is the Wing Chun elbow strike.

Pien jeung (slant palm) uses the palm heel, with the fingers pointed to the centerline, to strike the opponent with short explosive power.

Training includes the complete application of each point while standing, with steps, during *chi sao* (sticking hands) and with an opponent during *san sao* (separate hands). Also taught in the curriculum are the applications of the forty points on a *muk yan jong* (wooden dummy), practicing the Gu Lao points with *yee jee seung dao* (double knives), and pole exercises collectively known as the *luk dim boon gwun* (six-and-a-half-point pole).

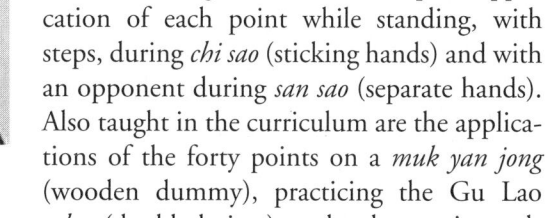

Cup da sao.

CONCEPTS AND PRINCIPLES

As with all Wing Chun systems, the Gu Lao forty-point system requires that the practitioner utilizes the principle of *"Lui lao hui soong; lut sao jik chung"* (As he comes, receive; if he leaves, escort. Rush in upon loss of contact with your opponent's hand).

Gu Lao Wing Chun employs the entire body and is a principle oriented martial art as opposed to a technique-oriented system. Timing and positioning are most important, along with the utilization of simple, direct economical movements in self-defense. A practitioner of the Gu Lao art is expected to learn the classical point, modify the technique according to circumstances, and combine a point with another point, while making use of *gerk faat* (footwork and foot maneuvers) (Figs. 10, 11).

Figure 10

Figure 11

Chu Sifu demonstrates *chuen sum gerk*, illustrating that in Gu Lao Wing Chun's footwork, every step can be a kick.

It is interesting to note that the Yuen Kay-San Wing Chun curriculum begins with many techniques similar to those of Gu Lao Wing Chun, and a trend of modern Wing Chun variations (e.g., jeet kune do) is to utilize many of the loose or separate techniques of Wing Chun kuen.

CONCLUSION

The Gu Lao Wing Chun system is a glimpse of the teachings of Wing Chun kuen in a *san sao* (free fighting) format. It is an ideal system to learn quick, simple, direct, economical movements for combat purposes.

CHAPTER 4

NANYANG WING CHUN KUEN

Southeast Asian Wing Chun is a generic term for all of the Wing Chun that was exported to Thailand, Malaysia, Singapore, and Indonesia from the southern provinces of China. Due to the lack of publicity, written records, and the shroud of secrecy surrounding the practice of Wing Chun, it is difficult to assess the actual number of Wing Chun sub-styles that are currently practiced in this area. In this respect, this chapter will only discuss one Southeast Asian sub-style of Wing Chun, the style of the late grandmaster Cao Dean (Cho Dak-On), which we shall hereafter refer to as Nanyang Wing Chun.

HISTORY AND DEVELOPMENT

According to verbal tradition as passed down by the late grandmaster Cao Dean, Nanyang Wing Chun was first conceived by Ng Mui, who thereafter passed the knowledge of the art to Yim Wing-Chun. Yim Wing-Chun then taught the style to Leung Bok-Chao. Leung as many did after him, looked down upon the "feminine" nature of Ng Mui's art and made the mistake of voicing his opinion. However, a sound thrashing by Yim Wing-Chun soon convinced him of the effectiveness of the system. They fell in love and were married.

Later Leung Bok-Chao was said to have made his way south to look for Jee Shim, who was rumored to be hiding among the Red Boat Opera performers as a cook. However, Jee Shim had already left and Leung stayed on to pass his knowledge of Wing Chun to the performers, notably Wong Wah-Bo, Leung Yee-Tai, Dai Fa Min Kam, Doo Ngan Shun (Snake Eyes Shun), Fa Jee Ming (Flower Mark Ming), and Sun Fook-Chuen. Later, Yim Wing-Chun was said to have made the journey south to join her husband and taught the opera performers personally.

The martial arts practiced by the Red Boat Opera performers were made up of the Wing Chun (Always Spring) forms of Jee Shim and the Wing Chun (Praise Spring) forms of Ng Mui. The opera performers lived a nomadic life, moving from one town to the next. Thus, it was only natural that they learned from, assimilated, modified, and incorporated other martial arts styles that they encountered in their travels. Coupled with this and the already expansive forms of Jee Shim, the number of forms in their syllabus was much more than what we would normally see today.

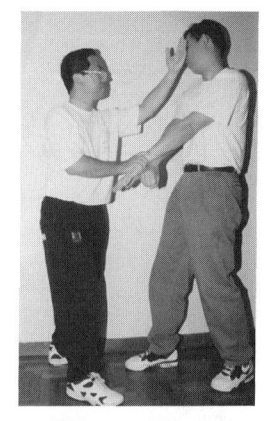

Latching an opponent's attack and countering with *fao jeung*.

The curriculum of the Red Boat Opera was said to consist of numerous different styles and sets. The forms which have been brought to Southeast Asia by Cao Dean include *siu nim tao* (small contemplation), *chum kiu* (seeking bridge), *biu jee* (thrusting fingers), *fa kuen* (variegated fist), *sui da* (random striking), *sam juen jeung* (three turning palms), *sam moon* (three gates), *fu hok seung ying kuen* (tiger-crane double shape fist), *tiet sin kuen* (iron wire), *fook fu jang* (subdue tiger elbows), *baat gwa sum* (eight trigrams center), *luk dim boon gwun sup sam cheung* (six-and-a-half-point pole thirteen spear), *yan jee dao* ("*yan*" character knives), and *chai mei gwun* (eyebrow level pole). There may have also been other forms of which we are not aware and have been lost to antiquity.

Overcoming an unexpected attack to the side using "eagle talon clawing ground," a variation of the *gum sao* technique.

Due to the sheer number of forms in the Red Boat Opera syllabus, not all students thereafter concentrated on learning all the sets with the exception of core forms such as *siu nim tao*. This may account for the diversity seen in the curriculum of today's Wing Chun traditions. Coupled with each succeeding generations' innovation, the face of Wing Chun has changed from its origins though the core forms have more or less remained intact (Figs. 1, 2).

It was a retired Painted Face Kam who by fate later passed on his knowledge to Cao Desheng (Cho Duk-Sang) and others. Cao Desheng came from a family of martial artists. For generations the Cao family had produced instructors in Hung ga kuen (Hung family boxing). Cao Desheng was the first to venture outside the family art. Cho Dak-Sang then handed on the mantle to Cao Dean and Cao Dewen (Cho Dak-Man).

Cao Dean, a native of the province of Guangdong, had earlier migrated to Malaya (known today as Malaysia) in the 1900s in search of a living. At the turn of the century China was undergoing turbulent changes and poverty was widespread. Migration from the Fujian and Guangdong region was high. As a young upstart, Cao got involved in a heated argument that turned into a fight. He thought he could win but Cao lost and was berated by the winner for his lack of skills. Cao vowed to learn martial arts and made his way back to Guangdong. There, he met the elder Cao and asked to be taken in as a student. Scores of years passed and Cao Dean matured into a young adult and more importantly a master of the art of Wing Chun.

An application from the Nanyang Wing Chun opening salutation.

Cao Dean eventually made his way to Hong Kong and opened up a Wing Chun school there for enthusiasts. It was here that Cao made the acquaintance of Yip Man, who shared a common interest with him in Wing Chun. As both were from Guangdong, they had frequent discussions on Wing Chun.

When the finger of economic opportunities once again beckoned, Cao made his way to Malaysia for the second time. Cao, a qualified chef, ended up in the galleys of a kitchen dishing up Cantonese food. Before long, word of his Wing Chun skills got around and he was soon persuaded to open a class for beginners.

It was a matter of time before the classes expanded and culminated in the

Figure 1

Figure 2

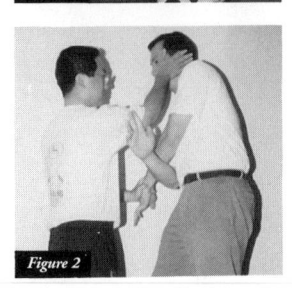

"Demon king waving fan" in form and in application. One of the older techniques preserved in Nanyang Wing Chun.

first Wing Chun school in the Malay peninsula. Classes in this practical art proved popular. There were, however, detractors mainly from the more traditional and established schools. Challenges were frequent but the art of Wing Chun prevailed and it was soon known as the fiercest martial art in Singapore. Martial artists who wanted to open schools were said to seek Cao's blessing. As was the case in Hong Kong during Yip Man's early teaching career, Cao's students also went out and made the school proud through informal challenge matches. Thus it came to pass that Wing Chun established a reputation in the peninsula as a martial art to be reckoned with.

As time passed and Cao grew old, he closed the doors on his teaching career. Cao Dean passed away in the 1980s at an age over ninety.

Cao's art was handed down to S.Y. Liu, among others. As a restless youngster, Liu lived, ate, and slept martial arts. His main preoccupation was testing the effectiveness of Wing Chun against other martial arts. Liu also taught on behalf of Cao. In the end, economic consideration forced Liu to put aside his much loved art to seek out a more realistic way of life. Today Liu is no longer actively involved in martial arts. He does not care to expose his knowledge of this potent art and only passed on his art to selected students. Today, Liu's Wing Chun is being spread by co-author Y. Wu in Singapore and Victor Leow in Sydney, Australia.

BASIC MOVEMENTS

The majority of Wing Chun systems are alike in that their basics revolve around the *siu nim tao* set. *Siu nim tao* provides training in pivoting, stepping, developing power through proper articulation of the joints, and familiarizes the neophyte with the basic hand strikes and kicks of Wing Chun, of which Nanyang Wing Chun has many. To effect the proper body mechanics and stability necessary to use these techniques, stances must be properly trained. There are three primary stances in Nanyang Wing Chun. *Sei ping ma* (natural adduction stance) is the most important stance in Nanyang Wing Chun as it develops stability and power. The natural adduction stance resembles a high version of the traditional low horse stance rather than the more familiar goat clamping stance. At the elementary level, the practice of adducting the legs provides training in generating an outward force from the *dan tian* area into the distance. This stance also allows for the equal use of both hands to move along the sagittal plane.

The *wang ma* (side stance) is a derivative of the adduction stance. It is the transition phase from the adduction stance to the side stance, necessary for the training of waist power and generating power along a curve.

The *gung jin ma* (bow and arrow stance) is for generating power by using the body. This stance is used for stepping forward as it protects the groin from an unexpected sudden front kick from the opponent.

Hand techniques are the most outstanding feature of Wing Chun. Here, I divide this discussion into anatomical hand weapons and generic hand techniques. There are seven anatomical hand weapons in Nanyang Wing Chun. They include:

Sae sao (snake hand; a.k.a. *biu jee*) is a finger jab used for training the force (*ging*) to reach the fingertips.

Fong ngan chui (phoenix-eye fist) is one of the two preferred fist types of Nanyang Wing Chun due to the damage that can be inflicted on an opponent through a sudden focusing of force into a tiny part of his body (akin to a knife stab). Phoenix-eye fist uses the bent tip end of the first metacarpal to issue a laser-like force that penetrates deeply due to the focusing of force into a small striking area.

Keung jee chui (ginger fist) is the other preferred fist type used in Nanyang Wing Chun. Its shape makes it suitable for striking target areas such as the throat or the ribs. The ginger fist resembles the conventional Siu Lam leopard fist in that the fingers are curled at the first metacarpals with the main striking area focused on the second finger.

Kam jang (covering elbow) is a devastating close range technique. Its importance lies in the training of extra articulation to generate power rather than just relying on the mass of the arm or the hardness of the elbow.

Chang jeung (spade palm) can be used with the palm facing down or palm facing forward depending on the chosen target.

Fao jeung (floating palm) is a whipping attack using the back of the hand to strike the opponent's nose.

Ying/fu jow (eagle/tiger claw) are the two major claw actions of Nanyang Wing Chun. Generally, the eagle claw is used for grabbing the opponent's throat but in techniques such as "cat washing face" the tiger claw is used. The presence of the latter is due to Jee Shim's influence on the historical development of Wing Chun.

There are twelve basic hand techniques in Nanyang Wing Chun. They include:

Tan sao (spread-open hand) is generally acknowledged as the "mother" technique from which the other techniques are derived. *Tan sao* energy is also the mother energy. At the elementary level, *tan sao* energy can be practiced as a lateral spiral energy. *Tan sao* varies in movement so that different energies can be practiced.

Fook sao (detaining hand) trains a spiral energy that is at once upward and to the side. A variation is to use folding to make a smaller planar triangle to create an energy that can simultaneously attack and be utilized as an invisible shield. The detaining hand can also be used proactively to intercept and attack the opponent's arm. *Fook sao* usage is not just confined to the wrist as is commonly seen but also the side of the palm.

Bong sao (wing arm) is commonly used as a side deflection technique. It can also be used to attack through the concept of *"bong"* energy rather than the technique itself. *Bong sao* energy is like a covering downward spiral force.

Taat sao (whipping hand) is an angular, backward jamming attack used to seal (or trap) an opponent's arms. It can either be performed with a jerking movement at the elementary level or with a smooth leading movement, very much like a caress but with a less than friendly intent.

Biu sao (darting hand) is also called *biu jee* and is a natural follow-up to *taat sao*. When the opponent falls forward as a result of the taat energy, the *biu sao* quickly darts forward to inflict a nasty strike to the throat or eyes.

Kaam sao (covering hand) is a technique used to redirect a centerline attack downward and back at the opponent using circular energy.

Gaun sao (cultivating hand) is a downward sweeping movement using the ulna bone to deflect the opponent's attack. *Gaun sao* is useful for opening up the opponent's front gate to expose his floating ribs to a ginger fist attack.

Gum sao (pinning hand) is a downward pressing action with the palm. It can also be an attacking technique to the side. *Gum sao* also goes by the colorful name of "eagle talon clawing ground." This variation of gum sao is powered by a wave-like energy.

Lan sao (barring hand) is a horizontal obstruction action using the forearm. *Lan sao* uses both a backward and forward spiral energy.

Kei chang (standing elbow) is a stopping movement performed with a sunken elbow and fingers pointing at an opponent. The standing elbow can be used with circular/spiral energy to unbalance the opponent.

Wu dip seung fei (butterfly palms) is one of the better known double palm strikes of Wing Chun. Leung Jan, the legendary "Wing Chun King Boxer," was said to be an adept at this attack. The use of butterfly palms is usually preceded by either an elbow breaking attack or a pulling or jamming movement to open up the opponent's defenses.

Mei lui chuen jaam (fair lady thread needles) is an attack with the fingers to the *ji chuan (*heart 1) acupoint. A variation is to use the

Figure 3   *Figure 4*   *Figure 5*

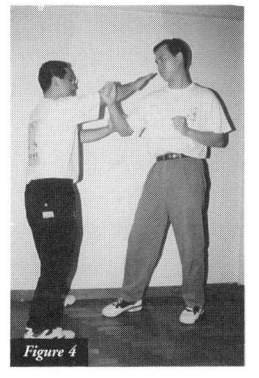

"Fair lady thread's needles" is shown in form and (Fig. 4) following a *biu sao* counter, (Fig. 5) in application.

tiger mouth of the hand to stop an advancing opponent by jamming his shoulder joint (Figs. 3–5).

There are eight kicks in Nanyang Wing Chun. They include:

Sao gerk (sweeping kick) is used to unbalance an opponent by sweeping out his legs from under him. This kick is normally used together with hand techniques to set him up.

Tarn gung gerk (spring leg) is a quick, medium-level jabbing kick using the heel. This kick is so-named because it is immediately retracted using the momentum of the kicking force (conservation of angular momentum) to whip the leg back. This action not only gives the kicking leg power but also prevents the kicking leg from being grabbed.

Bak hok chan sa (white crane shoveling sand, a.k.a. shoveling kick) is comprised of two movements. The first movement is a deflection using the shin. The second movement is a follow-up low side kick to the knees. The alignment of the *kwa* (knee and heel) with a twist-

Figure 6   *Figure 7*

Intercepting an opponent's front kick and deflecting the leg off the centerline before countering with white crane shoveling sand.

ing of the waist is what gives the shoveling kick its power (Figs. 6, 7).

Chuen sum gerk (center [heart] piercing kick) is not actually meant to be aimed at the heart as this would violate the rule of lifting the leg above waist level. Rather this kick is meant to be targeted at the groin area. The use of the character "heart" in the name of the kick does not refer to the target but is used to denote the action of getting to the heart of things (i.e., to penetrate deeply), using the curving force generated by the waist thrusting.

Fu mei gerk (tiger tail kick) is probably one of the most famous kicks in Chinese martial arts and is found in a number of styles. The tiger tail kick is a sneaky counter-attack used when the Wing Chun exponent has fallen to the ground with his back to the opponent. As the opponent rushes in for the kill, the tiger tail kick is unleashed to the groin area to inflict fatal injury.

Sam sing gerk (three star kick) is a kick that is used to protect the front and side gates from low kicking attacks, followed by a low heel or stamping kick to the knee.

Ding gerk (toe kick, a.k.a. nail kick) utilizes the tip of the shoes to target an opponent's groin. The toe kick is used when the opponent uses a stance that effectively shields his groin from a front snap kick.

Dang gerk (Stamping Kick) can either be used to prevent the opponent from retreating or to injure the sole of his foot by a short, sharp stamping action with your own foot.

FORMS AND TRAINING

Unlike the more compact systems of some Wing Chun styles, the art of Master Cao Dean, as passed to him by Master Cao Desheng from Dai Fa Min Kam, contains a great deal of forms and training methods. A unique characteristic of Nanyang Wing Chun forms are the use of common opening and closing movements. The opening movements contain the complex salutation said to be used by Wing Chun practitioners of the past to call for the overthrow of the Qing dynasty. Some of the forms that have been passed down to Nanyang Wing Chun are described below.

Siu nim tao (small contemplation) is the most important form in the Wing Chun syllabus of Master Cao. Beginners were normally taught a more simplified version whereas another version was taught at the end of the course. The latter small contemplation form was only released by Cao shortly before his retirement from active teaching. According to Cao, the small contemplation form was originally called the dictionary form and is the most advanced form in the Wing Chun

Figure 8 *Figure 9* *Figure 10* *Figure 11* *Figure 12*

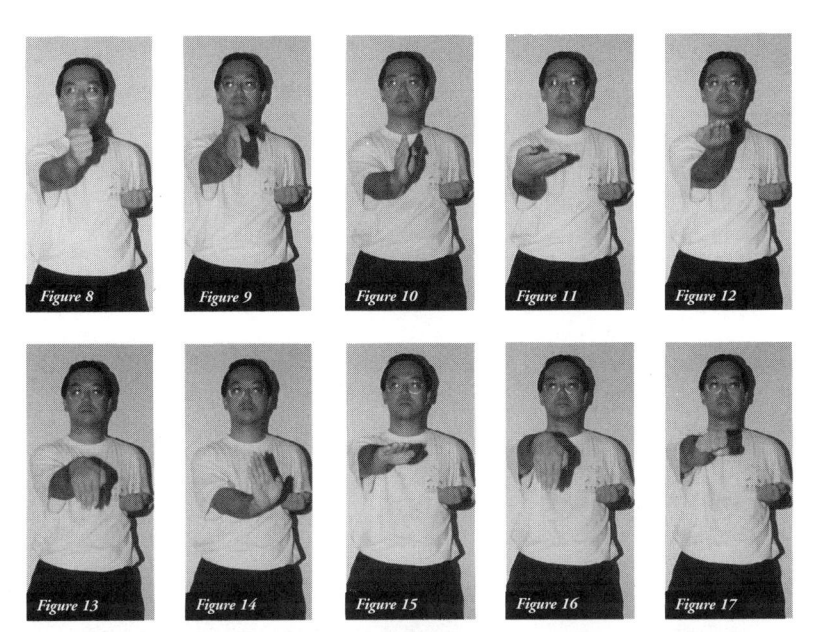

Figure 13 *Figure 14* *Figure 15* *Figure 16* *Figure 17*

The basic punching action of the *siu nim tao* which begins with (Fig. 8) vertical punch, and progresses through (Fig. 9) *ding sao*, (Fig. 10) *jut sao*, (Fig. 11) *hok sao*, (Fig. 12) *tok sao*, (Fig. 13) *huen sao*, (Fig. 14–15) *taat sao to biu sao* (performed 3 times), and (Fig. 16) *huen sao*, before (Fig. 17) the fist is held and withdrawn.

syllabus. Small contemplation form encompasses hand techniques, kicks, pivoting, and footwork (Figs. 8–17).

Chum kiu (scanning structure) is the intermediate form of Wing Chun and trains the practitioner to scan for the opponent's weak points. The scanning structure form works on the principle of curvilinear, rotational, and spiraling forces to attack the opponent's root structure (Figs. 18–31).

Biu jee (dart point), the third form of Wing Chun, is the paradoxical form. The dart point form uses the short to train the long. Important biomechanical articulations of the musculoskeletal structure are specially emphasized.

Fa kuen (variegated fist) contains elements of Jee Shim-type Wing Chun and is used to train the Wing Chun neophyte to move continuously from one movement to the next. The variegated fist form emphasizes the physical articulation of the eight characters formula of which the first four characters are *tao* (spit), *tun* (swallow), *fao* (rise), and *chum* (sink) (Figs. 32–41).

Sui da (random striking) contains techniques similar to Bak Mei kuen (White Eyebrow's boxing). Bak Mei was one of the five elders and we speculate that this form may be an indication that Bak

Mei also had a hand in the development of Wing Chun, alongside Ng Mui and Jee Shim. The random striking form concentrates on the use of mass transference as a means to cultivate linear, circular, lateral, and wrapping forces in addition to "leaking" (e.g., sneaking in punches).

Figure 18

Figure 19

Figure 20

Figure 21

Figure 22

Figure 23

Figure 24

Figure 25

Figure 26

Figure 27

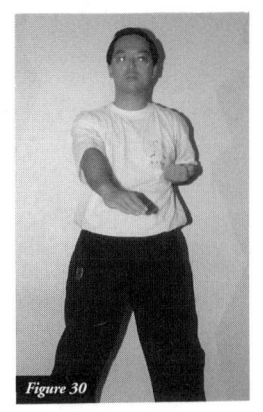

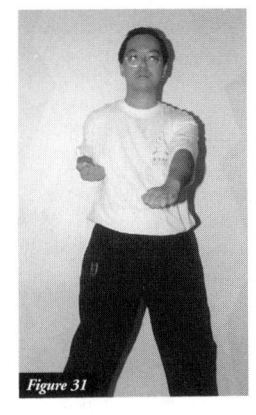

Figure 28

Figure 29

A section of the *Chum Kiu* form.

Figure 30

Figure 31

According to Master Liu, the essence of Wing Chun combat techniques lie in this form (Figs. 42, 43).

Muk yan jong is used to train the Wing Chun practitioner to maintain contact while flowing and moving non-stop around an opponent, while also maintaining correct placement of the arms and aligning the sagittal plane strategically.

Luk dim boon gwun (six-and-a-half-point pole) is used as an extension of the waist rather than just the hands to develop a more powerful springy force that is the result of projection along an extended path (Figs. 44–46).

Yan jee dao ("*yan*" character knives) is the short range weapon of Wing Chun. In using the knives, the knives become the hands and the hands become the knives. With this change in paradigm, the knives and hands are integrated. This concept is the basis for learning to release force from the body. The knives are so-called due to the unique method of holding them in some sections of the sets to form the Chinese character for "*yan*" (Figs. 47–49).

Figure 32

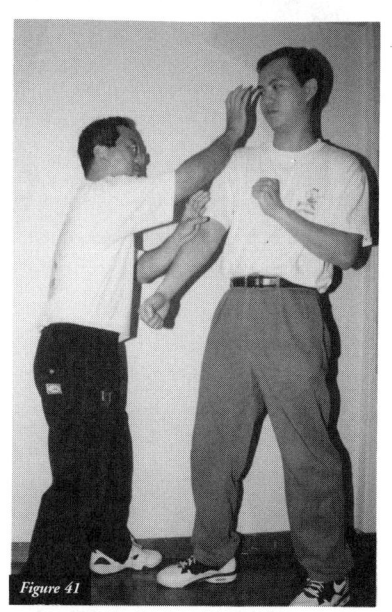

Figure 33

Figure 34

Figure 35

Figure 36

Figure 37

Figure 38

Figure 39

Figure 40

Figure 41

From *fa kuen*, (Figs. 32–38) a section of the form, (Fig. 39) assuming the "cat washing face" posture and (Fig. 40) applying it to counter an uppercut by pivoting and shooting the tiger claw into an opponent's face and then (Fig. 41) following-up by stepping forward to control an opponent's striking arm while simultaneously striking with a tiger claw to the face.

64

Figure 42

Figure 43

A *keung jee chui* posture from the *sui da* form and its application against a straight punch.

CONCEPTS AND PRINCIPLES

Nanyang Wing Chun is an art that is rich in concepts, principles, and paradigms. The following is an old saying that pretty much sums up the fighting philosophy of Nanyang Wing Chun: *"Yat jiu yat chak; Lay saat chak; Ng jiu ng chak; Wai seung chak"* (One block, one strike; You may not prevail; No [fixed] technique, no resistance; You prevail every time).

The implication of the first two stanzas is that reliance on techniques alone, especially blocking first and then counter-attacking, may not always work. Concurrent deflection and countering is preferable. The simple rationale is that usage of the first option may only result in the aggressor continuing his attack and the defender having to continue defending. The danger is that it is not really possible to continue blocking strike after strike without getting hit. Simultaneous attack and defense turns the table on the opponent and forces him to play the role of defender rather than attacker.

The second part stresses the importance of the ability to change and adapt in combat as a result of ever-changing circumstances and techniques used by different opponents. The importance of using energy in relation to neutralizing and issuing force is also implied. Energy cannot be seen, only felt. Hence, a technique can have numerous types of energy originating from different power sources depending on the concept used. It is easy to deal with a single technique using a single source of power, more difficult to handle a technique which can change into another technique, but very difficult-if not nearly impossible-to handle a technique with no apparent power source.

Planar positioning and alignment (PPA) is the core principle underlying the art of Nanyang Wing Chun. PPA is a more comprehensive principle than the centerline principle in its incorporation of horizontal, vertical, and oblique planes to act as shields for defense, and in which to wedge planar insertions for attack. In addition, PPA stresses the use of symmetrical and asymmetrical planar alignment to disrupt the opponent's power base through the use of minimal power.

Quadratic zones (QZ) are used as reference points to define the parameters for attack and defense. QZs can be on a major or minor scale, are not constant, and change according to the positioning of the technique.

Movements of the 6 1/2 point pole:

Figure 44

Biu gwun.

Figure 45

Tan gwun.

Figure 46

Saat gwun.

Triangulation projection (TP) underlies the basic concept for developing a stable stance. TP can also be applied to hand techniques to develop wedging power for entry techniques. At an advanced level, TP can be converted to multiple vortex-generated forces (MVF) for greater power.

The circle is the basis of a very powerful force in Wing Chun. Using power rings, circular energy can be manifested to concurrently deflect and return the attacking energy to an opponent. As with PPA, power rings can also be divided into the three basic categories of vertical circle, horizontal circle, and oblique circle. Circular energy can change into spiraling energy that wraps around the opponent's mother-line to destabilize the opponent, rendering him vulnerable to attacks. Circular and spiral energy (CSE) can further transform into MVF for greater variety of power.

Conservation of energy resources (CER) is conditional upon minimal muscular exertion and optimal biomechanical alignment. A body in work consumes energy and fatigues the body after a period of time, depending on the person's fitness and health. The more strenuous the work, the more muscles come into play, the faster fatigue sets in. This means that a person who is not fit is at a disadvantage when it comes to self-defense, a physical art. To overcome this and to give the average person an advantage, conservation of energy resources is a must.

Conservation of motion (CM) works concurrently with the principle of conservation of energy resources to optimize power while seeming to move very little relative to the opponent. The greatest of masters seem to move very little and with little effort. This is maximizing work with minimal energy.

The *dan tian* is traditionally considered the source of power in martial arts. Thus in practice, the Wing Chun

Figure 47
Chopping knives.

Figure 48
Slicing knives.

Figure 49
An application of chopping knives.

practitioner should follow the principle of *dan tian* projection (TTP) which is to let the force project out into the distance. TTP can work simultaneously with CSE, TP, and PPA.

By emulating a spring, the body can generate a force that can propel an opponent backwards. This can be done through the theory of compression (TC). By folding the relevant joints, a "springy" force can be produced. This is different from trying to generate force by creating a path of energy from the rear leg to the hand.

CONCLUSION

Nanyang Wing Chun, as a martial art that stresses practicality, naturally has a large repertoire of techniques ranging from striking and kicking to locking and throwing. Despite the wide ranging techniques, in the end Nanyang Wing Chun is a martial art form that is based on the use of subtle scientific, natural forces and energy. The techniques are but a means to express the forces and energy inherent in each of us and in nature.

Centuries ago, Mencius said: "I am great at cultivating my flood-like *qi*." Nanyang Wing Chun, through its forms, supplementary exercises, and interactive application exercises, seeks to develop the power of the spiral, the circle, the vortex, the pendulum, and the palindrome through emphasis on the body's power sources.

While power can corrupt, it can also develop positive character. Nanyang Wing Chun seeks to bring out the positive side in all of us by understanding ourselves, the people we come into contact with, our immediate surroundings, and the environment. In this way, we can not only become better martial artists but ultimately better people and good, responsible citizens.

Chapter 5

PAN NAM WING CHUN KUEN

While many styles of Wing Chun have left their roots in Foshan and journeyed to other parts of China, Hong Kong, Southeast Asia, and around the world, the Wing Chun preserved by master Pan Nam had, until only recently, remained in that fabled city. Brought to North America in the early 1990s by Pan Nam's last student, Eddie Chong (Chong Yin-Cheung) of Sacramento, California, the unique Wing Chun of Pan Nam is now available to a new generation of practitioners.

HISTORY AND DEVELOPMENT

According to Pan Nam Wing Chun traditions, the art that would become Wing Chun kuen began with the formation of the Tien Dei Hui (Heaven and Earth Society) anti-Qing revolutionary movement in the mid-1670s. The style itself was reportedly a special blend of techniques from Siu Lam (Shaolin or Young Forest), tai gik (taiji or great ultimate), ying jow (yingzhao or eagle claw), tong long (tanglang or preying mantis), gum gang jeung (jingangzhang or diamond, a.k.a. buddhist palms), kum na (qinna or seizing and holding), and other martial arts.

Lai Hip–Chi, Pan Nam's second Wing Chun teacher.

Between the end of the eighteenth and beginning of the nineteenth centuries, a twenty-second generation Siu Lam nun known as

Yat Chum Um Jee (Speck of Dust, Founder of Convent) established a convent on Hengshan in Hunan province. There, she began teaching the as yet unnamed style to carefully selected disciples. Among her students was a man nicknamed Tan Sao Ng (Spreading Arm Ng), the manager of props and costumes for a Hunanese opera company. Eventually (perhaps due to his revolutionary activities) Ng was forced to flee Hunan and ended up in Foshan, Guangdong. In Foshan, Ng began organizing the Hung Suen (Red Junk) Opera performers and founded the Hung Fa Wui Goon (Red Flower Union).

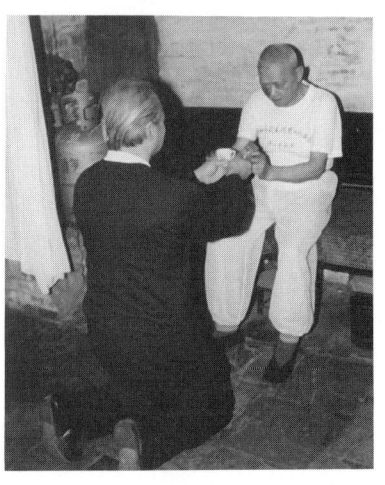

Chong Sifu offers Master Pan Nam the ceremonial cup of tea while asking to be accepted as his disciple.

The Red Junks were a hotbed of revolutionary activity and Tan Sao Ng taught his knowledge of traditional opera and martial arts to several of the performers. Among those who learned were said to have been Wong Wah-Bo (who played Mo-sang, the martial lead), Leung Yee-Tai (who played Mo-deng, the "female" martial lead), Dai Fa Min Kam (who played the "Painted Face"), and Lai Fook-Shun (who played Siu-Sang, the romantic lead). Eventually, the style practiced by the opera company revolutionaries became known as Wing Chun boxing. "Wing" came from the name of Chan Wing-Wah, one of the founders of the Heaven and Earth organization. Chun was formed from a combination of the characters for the three core words *tai* (great, meaning the Ming dynasty), *tien* (heaven, representing the Heaven and Earth Rebellion), and *yat* (sun, symbolizing the return of light). The three characters rendered together formed a shorthand revolutionary slogan meaning that only by overthrowing the Qing dynasty could freedom return.

Master Pan Nam and his last disciple, Eddie Chong (Chong Yin–Cheung), in Foshan ca. 1990.

During the early- to mid-nineteenth century Yip Man-Sun (the Qing general of Guangdong and Guangxi provinces), was sent to smash Lee Man-Mao, Chan Hoi, and their anti-Qing rebellions. In so doing, General Yip destroyed the opera theaters and outlawed the performances. This effectively ended the revolutionary movement until the 1860s when Sun Wah and Kwong Din-Hing formed the Baat Hop Wui Goon (Eight-Harmony Union) and re-opened the opera.

Between the early-1860s and mid-1870s, Wong Wah-Bo and Leung Yee-Tai left the opera and set up a school in Foshan where they passed along the Wing Chun style to Dr. Leung Jan. When Wong Wah-Bo later left Foshan, Leung Yee-Tai carried on the instruction of Leung Jan alone. At the same time Wong and Leung were in Foshan, Dai Fa Min Kam was engaged by Lok Lan-Gong to teach Lok and his nephew Wing Chun kuen.

During the last quarter of the nineteenth century, Dr. Leung Jan mastered the skills of Wing Chun and took on challengers from throughout China, eventually becoming renowned as the Wing Chun Wong ("King of the Wing Chun boxing"). By day, Leung Jan ran a pharmacy while at night he taught Wing Chun kuen to his son, Leung Bik, and to some of his close friends, including Lao Man-Kay, Dai San Siu (Big Mountain Siu) and Lo Kwai ("Chu Yuk" Kwai). Leung Jan's other son, Leung Chun, was said to have been born with extreme learning difficulties and to have died at a young age, never having learned martial arts. One of Leung Jan's most famous disciples was Chan Wah-Shun, known as Jiao-Chin Wah (Moneychanger Wah) because he worked in the market area converting money denominations. Chan Wah-Shun went on to have several Wing Chun disciples including his son, Chan Yiu-Min, and others such as Ng Siu-Lo, Ng Jung-So, Lui Yiu-Chai, Ho Han-Lui, Lee Jit-Man, Au Jaw-Ting, Lai Hip-Chi, and Yip Man.

Lai Hip-Chi was born in around 1898 to a wealthy family, and began following Chan Wah-Shun at the age of thirteen, becoming Chan's live-in apprentice and second-to-last student (although he started his studies at roughly the same time as Yip Man, he was a few months older and was thus considered the elder classmate).

Pan Nam presents Eddie Chong Sifu with a certificate.

Approximately half a year later, Chan Wah-Shun retired back to his hometown of Chen village in Shunde County. Rendered an invalid as the result of a stroke, the old moneychanger passed away a short time later.

Chan Yiu-Min, who became known as the Chut Sang Gwun Wong (King of the Pole of Seven Provinces), went on to teach the art to his children, Chan Ga-Wing, Chan Ga-Chai, and Chan Ga-Lim, and to students such as Jiu Chao and Jiu Wan.

Lai Hip-Chi continued his studies under Lui Yiu-Chai, one of Chan Wah-Sun's senior students. When Lai Hip-Chi was around twenty years old, he worked as the manager of a pawnshop and had occasion to attend the annual Pawnshop Association meeting. At the meeting, Lai noticed a wooden dummy off in the corner of the convention center. Rolling up his sleeves, Lai began to practice some techniques on it. This action drew the attention of Lok Lan-Gong's nephew, who by then was an old man in his seventies. From Lok's nephew, Lai learned more about the history and methods of Wing Chun kuen. Lai Hip-Chi passed along his Wing Chun kuen to several students including Pan Nam.

Master Pan Nam and Eddie Chong practice techniques at the Foshan Jing Wu Association.

Master Pan Nam and Eddie Chong engage in sensitivity training.

Pan Nam, known by the nickname Hak Min Nam (Black-Face Nam) due to a large facial birthmark, was born in 1911 and started studying the art of Hung ga kuen at the age of thirteen. In 1947, Pan Nam began to learn the Wing Chun style from his good friend Jiu Chao. Besides Pan Nam, Jiu Chao also taught Wing Chun to Jiu Ching, Jiu Sang, Gao Tong, Kwok Sing, and others.

In 1957, Pan Nam attended the Guangdong Provincial Martial Arts Competition and was introduced to, and became the student of, Lai Hip-Chi. Lai Hip-Chi had also taught the art to Hui Sam-Joy, Hung Mun, Yim Man, Yeung Sang, Yeung Dak, and others.

Lai Hip-Chi passed away in 1970 at the age of seventy-two and Jiu Chao passed away in 1972 in Zhongshan. Pan Nam continued teaching Wing Chun in the city of Foshan until his own passing in December 1995. Among his students were his sons, Pan Siu-Cho and Pan Siu-Lam, and students Lee Dak-Sang, Wong Jee-Keung, Lun Fao, Leung Chong-Ting, and Eddie Chong.

It was Eddie Chong, Pan's final student, who brought the art to the United States in the early 1990s. Through his articles and seminars, Chong has introduced the system to another continent of enthusiasts and helped ensure the preservation of Pan Nam's Wing Chun style.

BASIC MOVEMENTS

The techniques in Pan Nam Wing Chun are relaxed yet focused, creating a dynamic feeling and power. These techniques are described below.

The *yee jee kim yeung ma* ("*yee*" character pressing *yang* stance), which resembles the *sei ping ma* (square level horse) of classical Siu Lam, is the basic stance of Pan Nam's style. This posture provides a powerful foundation for strikes, great mobility and balance, and enhances the *hei (qi)* aspects of the system by properly aligning the three yang points on the sole of the foot. In this posture, the legs are opened to a medium distance and the toes point straight forward. The *bik ma* (pressing horse) also uses a 50/50 weight distribution and uses stepping movements, as opposed to dragging the rear leg to advance. In this position, the equal weight distribution promotes ease of movement in all directions.

The *jik chung chui* (centerline punch) in Pan Nam Wing Chun moves straight out from the shoulder, which is considered the centerline of the system. In the first form, *siu nim tao,* this punch is chambered in a vertical position; in later forms it is retracted along a horizontal plane.

Pan Nam Wing Chun practitioners always seek to develop a strong forearm to enhance the system's clawing and raking actions.

FORMS AND TRAINING

Pan Nam Wing Chun contains the three fist forms of *siu nim tao* (little idea), *chum kiu* (seeking bridge), and *biu jee* (darting fingers). Each form begins with an opening movement which symbolizes the revolutionary slogan: *"Fan Qing fu Ming"* (Overthrow

Figure 1

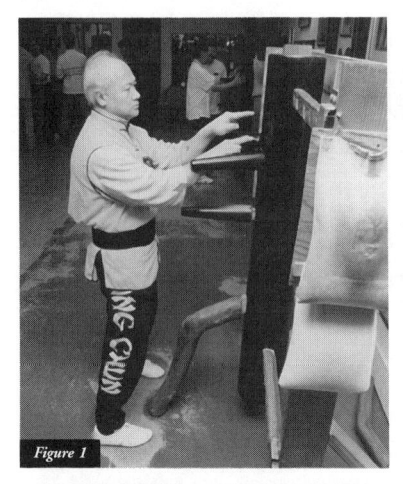

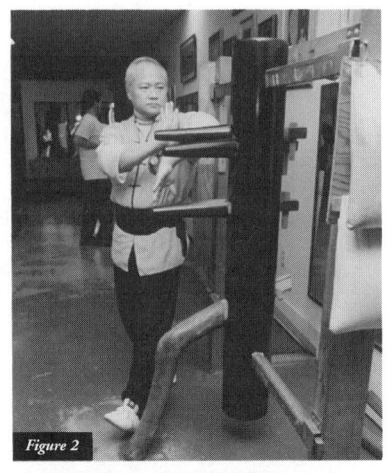

Figure 2

Figure 3

Figure 4

Eddie Chong Sifu performs movements from Pan Nam's wooden dummy set, including some of the unique finger–tip and claw-hand techniques of the system.

the Qing dynasty and return the Ming dynasty). Movements in the forms are executed at a slow, deliberate tempo, enhancing the cultivation of *hei* so important to the system. Each of the sets takes eight minutes to perform. Emphasis on the *huen sao* (circling hand) technique at the end of each section shows the characteristic eagle claw training, with each finger slowly gripping. This and several other techniques readily show the influences of great ultimate, eagle claw, preying mantis, seizing and holding, and other elements from which the style was synthesized.

Siu nim tao (little idea) teaches the basic stance, body structure, and hand techniques, combined with the breath. The idea of this form is to "internally train a breath of air and to externally train the muscle sinew and bones."

Figure 5

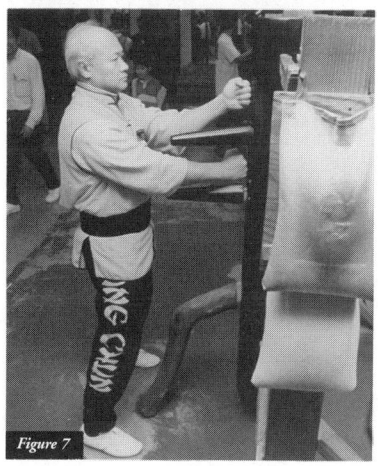

Figure 6

Figure 7

Figure 8

Chum kiu (seeking bridge) adds to this body shifting and body position displacement, combines movement with footwork, and introduces the ability to "bridge the gap and seek the opponent's bridges."

Biu jee (darting fingers) teaches many open-hand patterns and finger attacks with an emphasis on rotational power developed for the stance, waist, and torso.

Muk yan jong (wooden dummy) is an important training element of the Pan Nam style of Wing Chun. The dummy itself is composed of a round trunk, buried deeply in the ground, and augmented with two upper-level arms, a mid-level arm, and a low-level leg. The dummy allows the practitioner to develop the many punches and kicks of the Pan Nam style, as well as the important claws, grabs, and pressure point strikes of the system (Figs. 1–8).

Luk dim boon gwun (six-and-a-half-point pole) is between seven and nine feet long and is said to descend from the poles used to by the

Red Junk operators. It is held with arms fully extended and uses short power to transmit force along the pole and through the tip. A brief set, with nothing fancy in the way of movements, the long pole concentrates on practical fighting techniques.

Fu mei seung dao (tiger tail double knives) movements are contained in a rich, dynamic form with lively footwork and techniques performed in eight directions.

Ng jee mui (five petal plum) is used along with the three boxing forms to actively enhance the cultivation of *hei*. The *ng jee mui* is a set of five short *hei gung (qigong)* exercises which seek to develop the tendons, sinew, muscles, and bones, and promote a free circulation of energy throughout the body.

At yiu (pressing the waist) is a two-person exercise of Pan Nam's art that trains stance and balance. In this exercise, two people stand in *yee jee kim yeung ma* and hold onto their partner's elbows while keeping the hands perpendicular to the body. The partners try to unbalance each other without having to take a step.

Chi sao (sticking hands), in which a practitioner does not roll hands but simply searches for openings and seeks to control the opponent, is also drilled extensively. While engaged in *chi sao*, practitioners will utilize the entire repertoire of techniques in the system. They will further sharpen their knowledge of Wing Chun principles in application and develop better timing, positioning, distancing, and sensitivity to an opponent's attacks. While the forms and dummy set serve to give a practitioner the basic tools, *chi sao* teaches the changes, combinations, and permutations of the art.

CONCEPTS AND PRINCIPLES

Pan Nam Wing Chun embraces the saying *"Lui lao hui soong; lut sao jik chung"* (As the opponent comes, you receive; as he leaves you escort; upon loss of contact rush in).

Stepping methods include *ngao* (hook), *jum* (needle), *tarn* (spring), and *tek* (kick), and are methods of entry. In essence, *ngao* is to hook the opponent's leg to enter; *jum* is a short, needling jab of a kick to enter; *tarn* is to spring forward with fast footwork; and *tek* is to kick the opponent to enter. With regard to foot techniques, Pan Nam said, "Understanding movement and stillness, you'll know when to go. If you have it or not (control of the opponent) you'll know whether to advance or retreat."

Hand methods encompass *gaun* (cultivating), *lan* (obstructing), *tan* (spreading), *bong* (wing), *chi* (sticking), *mo* (touching), *tong* (press-

Chong Sifu demonstrates with some of his students.

ing), and *dong* (swinging). On the subject of sticking, Master Pan Nam said, *"Sao chi sao mo dei jo"* (When hands stick to hands, there is nowhere to go).

Kicking methods are composed of *chuen* (inch), *gwai* (kneel), *lau* (stir), *saat* (brake), and *chai* (stamp).

Chuen is a short-range close kick. *Gwai* is using the knee to knock into the opponent's leg. *Lau* is using the twisting motion of your leg when you do your Wing Chun stomp kick. *Saat* is to stomp on your opponent's foot, as in braking when driving. Chai is to stomp at the opponent's leg (Figs. 9–11).

CONCLUSION

Pan Nam Wing Chun promotes realistic fighting skills, brevity, flexibility, practicality, the free-flow of yin and yang, strength and suppleness, correct timing, the hitting of fatal spots, speed, and vigor. Rich in culture, it still includes apparent clawing, ripping, tearing and "dirty" fighting techniques, which may give us a glimpse back into the early days of Wing Chun kuen. These elements, when coupled with the *hei gung* training, create a powerful and effective form of Wing Chun and martial art system on the whole.

Chapter 6

PAO FA LIEN WING CHUN

刨花蓮永春拳

Pao Fa Lien Wing Chun, with its distinct history and development, and large syllabus of forms and weapons, is a unique and intriguing part of the Wing Chun tradition.

HISTORY AND DEVELOPMENT

Pao Fa Lien Wing Chun is said to have descended from the Siu Lam Jee (Shaolinsi or Young Forest Temple). During the eighteenth century, the temple was destroyed by the invading Manchurians, who had overthrown the Ming dynasty of the Han and established the Qing dynasty. Forced to flee and go into hiding, the survivors swore to resist the invaders and to train a new generation of students to aid in the rebellion. In order for them and their descendants to be able to recognize each other, they devised the revolutionary motto *"Wing yun chi jee; Mo mong Hon juk; Dai dei wui chun"* (Always speak with determination; Don't forget the Han nation; Again will return spring). When spoken, the motto would clearly identify their brethren. In order to facilitate its use and to help disguise its revolutionary nature from the Qing, the motto was eventually shortened to "Wing Chun" ("Always Spring"), and came to lend its name to their fighting methods.

Like much which occurred during that time, due to the secrecy of the revolutionaries and the conflicts which surrounded them, the exact evolution of the style has become lost. By the turn of the nineteenth century, however, the art had come to rest with, among others, a monk known as Dai Dong Fung (Great East Wind), who's true name has since been forgotten. A highly skilled martial artist and ardent supporter of the revolution, his actions soon made him a wanted man, forcing him to flee from arrest at the hands of the Qing.

Eventually settling in the region of Qingyuan, Guangdong, Dai Dong Fung was taken in and provided shelter by the Tse brothers, Gwok-Leung and Gwok-Cheung. Though Mandarins in the Qing government, the brothers bore no love for the invaders and hoped that one day they would be overthrown. Seeing in them good characters, Dai Dong Fung took them as his disciples and taught them his Wing Chun style.

When Dai Dong Fung left to journey back to the north, the Tse brothers adopted an infant named Lao Dat-Sang, and when the boy was nine years old, they began training him in the martial arts. As a youth, Lao Dat-Sang worked at his job doing pao-fa ("wood planing"). The planed wood chips would be boiled for sap that was used in the old days as hair tonic. Since the character for *"Dat,"* is similar to the character for *"Lien"* (Lotus, a female name), from time to time people would teasingly call him "Siu Lien" (Little Lotus). After a time, he became known by the nickname Pao Fa Lien (Wood-Planer Lien).

Lao Dat-Sang learned Wing Chun for over a decade and later moved to the town of Foshan to work as a treasurer in a local establishment. Even though he was very quiet, and did not demonstrate his Wing Chun, word soon got around that he was highly skilled in the martial arts. Following a thirty-year exile abroad (resulting after Lao accidentally killed a man named Pan in a knife duel), Lao returned to Foshan and accepted a few students. Chu Chong, said to have been born just before the turn of the twentieth century, was fortunate to have become one of Lao Dat Sang's disciples, accepted when Lao was already over seventy years old.

Mok Poi–On Sifu, disciple of Chu Chong, demonstrates outside changing on the wooden dummy.

Chu Chong worked diligently at his Wing Chun and managed to grasp the true essence of the style. Later, Chu moved with his family to Hong Kong where he set up an osteopathy clinic. In Hong Kong, Chu Chong's style came to be called Pao Fa Lien Wing Chun, in order to honor his teacher and to distinguish it from other versions of the art which were already being taught in Hong Kong.

Chu Chong passed along Pao Fa Lien's Wing Chun to his sons,

Chu Wing-Jee and Chu Ping, and to Mok Poi-On who helped make the art known around the world.

BASIC MOVEMENTS

In the beginning, Pao Fa Lien stresses linear motions, but as time and training progress it begins to emphasize more freestyle interpretation.

Footwork takes precedence in Pao Fa Lien Wing Chun. The style favors constant movement and turning to probe for weaknesses in an opponent's defense. Stances include the *yee jee kim yeung ma* (goat pressing stance). This is complemented

Mok Sifu performs another movement on the wooden dummy, this one showing Pao Fa Lien's characteristic T–step.

with stances like *gung ma* (bow stance) which uses an even weight distribution, *diu ma* (hanging stance), the characteristic *chut sing bo* (seven star step, a.k.a. *hao jaw bo*) which has the front leg resting lightly only upon its heel, and many others. Footwork includes *cheung sam bo* (long-robe steps) which use *gung ma* in a triangular step, *juen bo* (turning steps), *huen bo* (circling steps), and others including highly specialized forms such as *baat gwa bo* (eight triagrams step), found only in the weapons sets. Kicking methods, which are aimed to strike below the waist, include a variety of front, side, and specialized sweeping movements. Adding to these are strikes utilizing the knees and hips.

Pao Fa Lien Wing Chun is rich in upper-body techniques. The primary fist technique is *yat jee kuen* ("*yat*" character fist) which is issued in a relaxed manner, with power focused through the third knuckle. Additional fist strikes include the *bien chui* (whipping punch) backfist, the *jong chui* (hooking punch), and the *pao chui* (cannon punch) uppercut, which cover all basic angles. The style also contains numerous methods of striking with the palm and fingers including *chit jeung* (slicing palm), *dai jeung* (low palm), and *biu jee* (darting fingers). Strikes are also issued with the elbows and shoulders. Principle arm movements include the *tan sao* (spreading hand), *bong sao* (wing hand), *pak sao* (slapping hand), *kao sao* (detaining hand), and *jut sao* (choking hand), among others.

FORMS AND TRAINING

Pao Fa Lien Wing Chun has a much larger syllabus then most other styles of Wing Chun. It is composed of ten empty-hand sets, four wooden dummy sets, and over a half-dozen weapon sets.

Each of the ten empty-hand sets is unique and comprise over 100 movements a piece. The first form, *siu nim tao* (little idea) begins in the static *yee jee kim yeung ma* stance but changes to the moving *cheung sam bo* midway through. It also includes other footwork such as the style's trademark T-shape steps. *Chum kiu* (seeking bridge) is the longest of the Pao Fa Lien Wing Chun forms and along with *biu jee* (daring fingers), completes the basic level forms training. The mid-level forms include *tut sao* (freeing arm), *dui sao* (chopping arm), *bin kuen* (whipping fist), and *sup jee* (*"sup"* character), each tending to focus on the actions of the technique after which it is named. *Jin kuen* (arrow punch), *jin jeung* (arrow palm), and *juk san* (side body) comprise the advanced-level forms.

Four wooden dummy sets are included in Pao Fa Lien Wing Chun. Each set is different and serves to train different elements. The *noi jong* (inside dummy) and *ngoi jong* (outside dummy) forms develop techniques primarily devoted to attack and defense from the interior gate and exterior gate respectively. The *gong jong* (hard dummy) form trains external power, while the *yao jong* (soft dummy) form promotes internal power. Pao Fa Lien Wing Chun also contains unique dummies and sets meant to train the pole and the knives.

A tiger tail movement from the *luk dim boon gwun* techniques.

Weapon sets in Pao Fa Lien style focuses on the *luk dim boon gwun* (six-and-a-half-point pole) and the *mor poon seung dao* (millstone double knives). The pole and knives are practiced through their respective sets, two-person sticking drills, and unique wooden dummies.

The *luk dim boon gwun* is performed with a pole of over seven feet in length. It derives its name as it is a single ended weapon (only one end of the pole is used for combat). Thus, like a clock at the 6:30 position, the pole projects from the user in only one direction (although the hands and body can move to attack or defend at any angle). The pole methods contain such primary sets as *fu mei* (tiger tail) and *sin mien* (fanning).

The double knives include techniques that spin to cover all directions. This resembles a millstone as it turns to grind grain, and is the reason why the form is so named. In contrast to many southern systems, the Pao Fa Lien knives always project outward and are never flipped backwards. The millstone knives contain over 200 movements, including *baat jaam dao* (eight chopping knives) and *seung chum dao* (double sinking knives) and utilize very nimble footwork. The techniques of the double knives closely match the methods of the hands and include such motions as *pak* (slapping), *kao* (detaining), *jut* (choking), *chit* (slicing), and *biu* (darting).

In addition to these, sets are taught which deal with the use of the sup sam yei yun bin (thirteen section whip), siu lung gim (scholar's sword), dai pa (trident), Kwan dao (Kwan's knife), among other weapons.
The *chi sao* (sticking arms) practice of Pao Fa Lien more closely resemble the *tui sao* (pushing hands) of tai gik kuen (taijiquan) than the *luk sao* (rolling hands) seen in other Wing Chun branches. Adherence and sensitivity training begins with circular arm work from a stationary position. Leg conditioning is introduced next, and eventually the hands and legs are used in combination. The last level of training is free style, where partners spontaneously apply their knowledge without pre-set patterns.

CONCEPTS AND PRINCIPLES

Pao Fa Lien Wing Chun uses the *tao* (spit), *tun* (swallow), *fao* (rise), and *chum* (sink) body structure. The art is embodied in the eight principles of *tui* (push), *mo* (touch), *tong* (press), *dong* (swing), *chi* (stick), *na* (adhere), *lien* (continue), and *jui* (follow). The first four deal with contacting and redirecting the opponent's limb and body. The last four cover the establishment and maintenance of such contact.

CONCLUSION

Although Pao Fa Lien Wing Chun has always been a closely guarded style, taught to only a handful of dedicated practitioners, in the last few decades it has begun to step into the light and show itself to the world. Through Mok Poi-On's articles and seminars, it was introduced to readers and attendees around the world, and hopefully the art will remain strong and available for generations to come.

Chapter 7

HUNG SUEN WING CHUN KUEN

紅船永春拳

The Hung Suen Wing Chun kung-fu system dates back over two hundred years to the Siu Lam Temple. As a result of the political atmosphere of the times, this branch of Wing Chun has never been made public or taught outside its direct lineage. Instead, it was handed down in secrecy from family member to family member.

HISTORY AND DEVELOPMENT

From 1644 to 1911, the Manchurians ruled China in a period known as the Qing dynasty. Early in the 1700s, the Manchurians became concerned about the Siu Lam Temples' rebellious activities and their continued development of the fighting arts. Under the decision to eliminate the threat of these rebels and their leaders, the Manchurians attempted to exterminate the Siu Lam monks to prevent them from spreading their martial arts skills and knowledge. Eventually, both Siu Lam Temples were burned and destroyed.

According to Hung Suen Wing Chun tradition, prior to the destruction of the temples, a comprehensive advanced martial art system known as Wing Chun was developed. Wing Chun was formulated through generations of Siu Lam knowledge and experience. As with all advanced Siu Lam knowledge, Wing Chun was conducted under a "silent code." This meant that in order to prevent abuse, it was passed down to only a few chosen disciples and was never documented.

With such a hidden past, we now rely heavily on the direct teachings of the elders for historical material. As told by teacher to student, two Siu Lam monks escaped the Manchurian massacres and were able to keep the Wing Chun system alive. One of these monks was the twenty-second generation Siu Lam grandmaster, Yat Chum

Dai Si. The other monk was named Cheung Ng. Before his death, grandmaster Yat Chum Dai Si passed on his high level Wing Chun knowledge to Cheung Ng.

In order to keep his identity and Siu Lam background hidden from the Manchurian government, Cheung Ng joined the Red Boat Opera Troupe. The name was given to this organization of talented stage performers who traveled in red boats. Accomplished in kung-fu and gymnastics, they formed their own association called the Hung Fa Wui Goon (Red Flower Union). Utilizing heavy make-up, elaborate costumes, and stage names, the Red Boat Opera Troupe was Cheung Ng's safest refuge.

Cheung Ng became known in the opera troupe as Tan Sao Ng (Spread-Out Arm Ng) from his skillful use of the Wing Chun maneuver *tan sao* to subdue others during challenges. His level of skill allowed him to use one *tan sao* move to represent over a thousand moves. He demonstrated that a basic technique such as *tan sao* must be fully understood, in concept and application, prior to the next thousand techniques. After learning the next thousand techniques, then they all become one again.

Harsh Manchurian actions created such distrust among the people that they resulted in the formation of underground organizations or secret societies such as the Heaven and Earth Society and the White Lotus Society. Within a secret society, the identity of the leaders, members, and activities were known only to few within the society itself.

One of the Red Boat Opera Troupe actors by the name of Hung Gun Biu (Red Bandanna Biu), was a secret society leader and brought Tan Sao Ng into the organization. The safety of the opera troupe combined with the security of the secret society is what allowed Ng to spread his Wing Chun knowledge in confidence.

As a trusted leader, Hung Gun Biu became one of Ng's closest disciples. However, in order to protect the system's origin and the identities of Yat Chum Dai Si and Tan Sao Ng, a story was created. It was said that a Siu Lam nun named Ng Mui taught the martial arts to a young woman named Yim Wing-Chun. As Yim Wing-Chun taught it to others, the system became known as Wing Chun kung-fu. Many versions of the story exist around the world today. However, the name "Yim Wing Chun" also has a different and special meaning. "Yim" can be translated to mean protect, prohibit, or secret. The term "Wing Chun" referred to the Siu Lam Wing Chun Tong (Always Spring Hall). Thus, "Yim Wing Chun" was actually a code, meaning the secret art of the Siu Lam Wing Chun Hall.

Hung Gun Biu became one of the first generation disciples to learn Wing Chun, outside the Siu Lam Temple. The other opera troupe members who learned Wing Chun from "Tan Sao" Ng also had the obligation to protect the origin of the system. These other first generation disciples included Wong Wah-Bo, Leung Yee-Tai, Dai Fa Min Kam (Painted Face Kam), Lo Man-Gong, Siu-Sang Hung Fook, and Gao Lo Chung (Tall Man Chung). Based on their individual understanding and degree of training in Wing Chun, these disciples, all previously trained in other martial art styles, may have passed along their skills with inherently different emphases.

Hung Gun Biu's lineage became known as Hung Suen (Red Boat) Wing Chun and followed a tradition to pass down the full system only to family members who took the traditional and ceremonial Siu Lam vow of secrecy. The system's lineage shows that Hung Gun Biu taught his relative, Cheung Gung who passed it down to his great nephew, Wang Ting. Wang Ting taught his son, Dr. Wang Ming, of Saiquan, China. Dr. Wang Ming taught the entire system with its original concepts to only four disciples. One of these disciples was Garrett Gee (Chu King-Hung).

Garrett Gee was born into a multi-generational martial arts family in the Guangdong province of southern China. His family kung-fu lineage is from Sun Lutang and Fu Zhenxiong (one of the Five Northern Tigers of China). His father, Peter Chu (Chu Kim-Ho) is a well-known Wudang grandmaster.

Garrett Gee Sifu, one of Dr. Wang Ming's four disciples.

Garrett Gee began his martial arts training with his father at the age of five. Throughout his early years, he studied the Wudang systems including taiji and bagua. He also trained in the Jing Wu School as well as the Siu Lam systems and became proficient in the use of many weapons.

At the age of thirteen, Garrett Gee started his Hung Suen Wing Chun training directly under Master Wang Ming. In 1975, when he completed his training, he moved to the United States where he has been teaching for over twenty years. In addition to being a sixth-generation Hung Suen Wing Chun disciple, he teaches multiple weapon forms and application, and his family's Wudang system.

FORMS AND TRAINING

There are four forms in Hung Suen Wing Chun. The first form, *siu nim tao* (little idea), emphasizes proper positioning and alignment of individual hand and arm extensions from the body, along with use of *hei (qi)* energy. It represents the basic tools needed to learn the rest of the system. The second form, *chum kiu* (destroy the opponent's structure), emphasizes the most advantageous way to deal with an opponent in a combat situation. Literally translated, *chum kiu* means "sinking the bridge." However, what "sinking" meant to the Siu Lam was to "destroy." The term "bridge" represented the structure of the opponent to be destroyed. Thus, this system understands *chum kiu* to mean "destroy the opponent's structure." The third form, *biu jee* (thrusting fingers), is a dynamic finger striking form which concentrates on attacking an opponent's vital points. The fourth form is taught in conjunction with a *muk yan jong* (wooden dummy). It teaches correct positioning of angles and helps develop power. Wooden dummy training starts in the first level of the system. It is recommended that the novice hit the wooden dummy with force in order to condition the body. However, in the more advanced levels, hitting with excessive force is not stressed.

Garrett Gee Sifu is shown here applying *lop da*.

Additional training activities unique to the system are chi sao, *chi gerk*, and body conditioning exercises. The first two exercises develop balance and sensitivity necessary to detect and redirect incoming energy (applied with arms and legs). Body conditioning involves sand bag training and the use of different types of dit dat jao (herbal medicine) for strengthening and healing.

Specific footwork training incorporates the underlying principles of the six basic stances which maintain weight distribution of fifty-percent on each leg for maximum mobility. The most basic stance, with feet facing forward, is called *yee jee ma* (*"yee"* character horse). This stance allows maximum mobility by not turning the toes inward and is different from a stance used by others called *yee jee kim yeung ma* (pinching goat horse). When in motion the feet step in a natural fashion rather than slide and the body does not lean in any direction in order to maintain one's center of gravity.

In the system's more advanced levels weapons training is taught and includes the six-and-a-half-point staff and double butterfly knives. The butterfly knives are practiced with the wooden dummy in an advanced weapon training form.

All movements contained in the forms have specific training value and combat applications. Prior to speed and power, this system emphasizes precise angles, energy, and principles. Herein lies the advantage for one who is slower or less powerful to defeat one with more power and/or speed.

There are six specific training categories with ten progressive levels of development in Hung Suen Wing Chun. Each level provides specific knowledge and understanding, using sensitivity with internal and external energy. Training is done in the following six categories:

1) Individual (one man) training methods include: the three forms *(sui nim tao, chum kiu, bui jee)* and wood dummy form taught with two concepts (eight directional; space/time factors with specific angles beyond the eight directions).

2) Two-man (partner) training methods include: *don chi sao* (single sticking arms); *seung chi sao* (double sticking arms); blindfolded *chi sao; chi gerk* (sticking legs); twelve specific combination sparring drills; five stages of combat (pre-contact, contact, exchange, tracing, and retreating; and the twelve specific basic action training techniques for single-action defense.

Garrett Gee Sifu leads a class in the practice of *chum kiu*.

3) Assisted training methods include: *chin chang qigong* (1000 paper drilling/soft palm training internal energy); bamboo section training (which includes ground fighting); iron palm conditioning; weapons training (butterfly knives and staff) (Figs. 1–4); *qigong* with *siu nim tao* breathing; combat strategy including inch power (for short range), *chi sao* (for sensitivity and reflexes), the thirty-six ways of *chum kiu* change utilizing six types of footwork (neutral, side neutral, angle-in forward stance, exchange, attack, and retreating) combined with each of the six gates (left and right upper, middle, and lower); wooden dummy and *chum kiu* strategy and footwork; and concept analyses supported by science and physics.

Figure 1

Figure 2

Figure 3

Figure 4

Garrett Gee Sifu demonstrates butterfly knives vs. long pole.

CONCEPTS AND PRINCIPLES

The root of Hung Suen Wing Chun lies within its distinctly unique concepts and principles. Full understanding of the concepts and principles is imperative in order to perform the system with maximum efficiency and effectiveness. Any individual interpretations or attempts to combine the system with other styles will deviate from these concepts and, therefore, render the system ineffective (Figs. 5–7).

Training entails how to position oneself to create an advantage over an opponent while maintaining center of gravity. Upon initial contact with an opponent, focus is on intercepting the attack and feeling the energy. Distortions in the opponent's position can then be detected which allow for attack of strategic targets to destroy the opponent's structure. A few of the more common principles are outlined below.

- Maintaining center of gravity, upper and middle gates
- Follow/protect the centerlines (vertical and horizontal)
- Awareness of six gates and focus points (som guan, yun jung, tan jung, dan tian)

- Application and coordination of six types of footwork
- Safety zones and zone control concept, location, and application
- Maintaining of optimal fighting range
- Maintain true timing with simultaneous attack and defense (without additional body adjustments)
- The concept and application of *liu lao hoi soon* and *lut sao jik chong*
- Ten levels of the three dimensions (defined viewpoints of angles and areas)
- Angle-in attack and defense for optimal position
- Basic defensive and offensive action in which specific techniques are used for specific attacks. These are considered "true" techniques which are always true for each situation. For example, bong sao is only used for a straight punch and never against a round punch, as this would violate the principle of following/protecting the centerline.

Figure 5

Figure 6

Figure 7

Garrett Gee Sifu practices free sparring.

CONCLUSION

Hung Suen Wing Chun is a clear and complete combat system unique unto itself. It is more important to understand the underlying concepts, principles, and theories of the system rather than the individual techniques. The development of position, timing, and energy flow of the practitioner are the most important aspects to fully understand and implement the system. This can only be fully appreciated and learned by a dedicated and serious student.

The beauty of the system is the depth of its simplicity. The value of the system is in the knowledge of how to deal with energy which can be applied in all aspects of one's daily life. The strength of the system lies in the fact that no additions or subtractions to the existing concepts, principles, and theories of the system are necessary.

Chapter 8

JEE SHIM WING CHUN KUEN

Jee Shim Wing Chun (also romanized as Chi Sim Ving Tsun) descends from the fabled Jee Shim, abbot of the Siu Lam (Shaolin) Temple. When Siu Lam was destroyed by the Manchurians, Jee Shim fled and hid amongst the Hung Suen Hay Ban (Red Junk Opera Company), disguising himself as a cook. One day, a fierce bully nicknamed Wong Lao Fu (Tiger Wong) came to the Junks to extort money. The opera performers, with skills geared more toward spectacular demonstration then real combat, were not able to defend themselves and Jee Shim was forced to take matters into his own hands. After easily dispatching the troublemaker, Jee Shim revealed himself to the performers and began to teach them his Siu Lam art, Wing Chun kuen (Always Spring boxing). The origin of Jee Shim's art does not remain as obscure or controversial as other histories of Wing Chun, as it simply descended from the Shaolin temple.

HISTORY AND DEVELOPMENT

Jee Shim Wing Chun is an old Chinese martial and healing art. The knowledge of the famous Siu Lam monastery is the nucleus of the system. This system uniquely combines the theories of martial arts and traditional Chinese medicine. Oral traditions of Jee Shim Wing Chun discuss legends of Bodhidharma (Dat Mor in Cantonese; Da Mo in Mandarin). According to these traditions, Bodhidharma left India and in 520 A.D. arrived at the Siu Lam monastery in China. Bodhidharma invented the basics of both Shaolin boxing and Wing Chun while contemplating questions of wholistic life, body awareness, and the way to generate energy, power, and master aggressiveness.

To this day, Jee Shim Wing Chun practitioners still celebrate the "birthday" of Bodhidharma.

In Siu Lam a special hall was built in which only the most experienced monks met over the centuries to improve and refine their kung-fu. The hall was either named Wing Chun Dien (Everlasting Vitality Hall) or Wing Chun Tong (Forever Springtime Hall). The martial art and *qigong* exercises taught in this hall became known as Wing Chun kuen (Always Spring Hall boxing).

For the Shaolin monks, the direct experience of reality was most important. Their Chan Buddhist philosophy dictated a return to a natural and simple existence. This stood in contrast to the philosophy of fighting styles which where taught outside of the temple. This was why in the Wing Chun hall only fighting concepts were collected which were truly simple and directly functional.

Because of treason against the Qing dynasty government, the Siu Lam temple was destroyed in the 18th century. The Siu Lam Abbot Jee Shim Sim Si escaped with other monks and became a cook on the Red Boat, using a pseudonym. The Red Boats were the ships of a Chinese opera group, which sailed form town to town entertaining the people. In legends of the Jee Shim Wing Chun circles, a brutal fighter of this time, named Wong Lao Fu (Tiger Wong), tried to extort protection money from the opera troop, giving them one day to pay up. If they refused to pay him, he threatened to destroy their boat. The opera troop, under the direction of Wong Wah-Bo, were desperate as they had no money and could not protect themselves; they did not know fighting kung-fu, only opera kung-fu. As their deadline came, the members of the Red Boat feared their end was near.

Jee Shim Wing Chun master Cheung Kwong.

Jee Shim, until then regarded only as a crazy cook, faced up to Tiger Wong. Wong did not take the cook seriously and tried to grab his neck with an tiger-hand technique. Jee borrowed Wong's energy and immediately broke two of his fingers. Jee advised Wong to stop the fight since he would have no chance of winning. Wong boiled with rage as an elderly, simple cook humiliated him in public. With fast and brutal chain punches Wong tried to gain victory over the cook. Jee Shim merely dodged Tiger Wong's blows and then locked his arms and legs with *kum na (qin-na)* joint locking techniques. The more Tiger Wong moved, the more he injured himself. Tiger Wong realized that he was confronting a true kung-fu master and gave up the fight.

A rare photo of the disciples of Jee Shim Wing Chun. Left to right: Way Yan, Lo Chiu-Wan, Chu Chong-Man, Tam Kwang, Dong Yik.

The members of the red boat were inspired to learn kung-fu from their cook. Abbot Jee Shim Sim Si revealed his true identity and taught the opera group. Because he was one of the most persecuted men of his time, his students had to promise to never mention his name. Many legends were invented regarding the history and development of Wing Chun to protect the identity of Master Jee Shim Sim Si. Only the Wing Chun masters who learned the entire system from their master where taught its true history.

Chu Chong-Man—The iron fist of wing chun.

Jee Shim's style was passed along to Wong Wah-Bo and Sun Kam (also known as Dai Fa Min or Painted Face Kam). Some accounts hold that Sun Kam learned directly under Jee Shim, while others maintain he was a student of Wong Wah-Bo.

While in Foshan acquiring new costumes, Sun Kam encountered a belligerent young tailor's apprentice named Fung Siu-Ching. After a quick lesson in manners, and a short probationary period, Fung became Kam's kung-fu student. Fung Siu-Ching later assisted Sun Kam with his opera makeup and learned the Wing Chun art. Later, Fung became a bounty hunter and marshall, and passed along his knowledge of Jee Shim Wing Chun kuen to many, many students including his son Fung Ting, as well as Dong Suen, Ma Jung-Yiu, Dong Jit, Lo Ying-Nam, and Lo Kai-Tong. As a result, Jee Shim Wing Chun has spread to various countries such as Thailand, Vietnam, Singapore, and Indonesia. Upon retiring at the age of seventy-one, Fung Siu-Ching took on a last disciple named Yuen Kay-San, and taught him privately at Yuen's home. Fung passed away at the age of seventy-three.

In Foshan, several of Fung's students provided local villages with protection against bandits. Around the year 1930, these students taught the famous Lo brothers, Chiu-Wan and Hong-Tai. Dong Jit passed the art on to Chu Chong-Man, who eventually moved to Macao where he became known as Chu "The Undefeatable" or the "Iron Fist of Wing Chun." Chu was a Chinese doctor by profession and did not actively teach students.

Dong Suen, who gained the title Cheung Gwun Wong (King of the Long Pole), took Pak Cheung and his son, Dong Yik, as disciples. Pak Cheung resided in Foshan, China. Dong Yik went to Hong Kong to actively teach the Wing Chun system. Lo Chiu-Wan relocated to Hong Kong where he taught his art to a wealthy friend named Way Yan (Wei En).

Desiring to preserve Jee Shim Wing Chun, Way went on to study with Lo Hong-Tai, Dong On, Dong Yik, and Chu Chong-Man, who became his close collaborator. These five studied and practiced Wing Chun together in Dai Duk Lan, a shipping dock in Hong Kong. To Jee Shim Wing Chun practitioners, Dai Duk Lan is revered as the place where these five masters were able to research and refine their art in relative secrecy. Dai Duk Lan invited Wing Chun masters from all over to visit and train. It is known amongst Jee Shim Wing Chun practitioners that Yip Man visited Dai Duk Lan to exchange

Andreas Hoffman and the late master Pak Cheung.

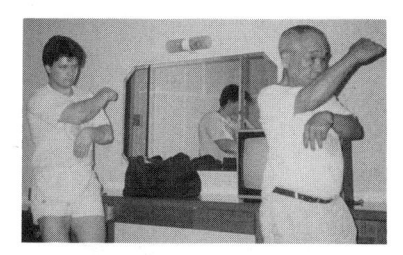

Personal instruction from master Pak Cheung.

Andreas Hoffman performing *bai si* to grandmaster Way Yan as his sifu Cheng Kwong looks on.

concepts with Chu Chung-Man, his distant relative. Dai Duk Lan provided the first hanging style wooden dummy in Hong Kong. Previously, all wooden dummies were buried into the ground and free standing.

Among Way Yan's students are Lau Chi-Lung and Cheng Kwong. Cheng Kwong passed the art on to Andreas Hoffmann of Bamberg, Germany. Hoffman later went on to research the Jee Shim Wing Chun kuen with his *si gung* (grand teacher), Way Yan and Way Yan's *si suk* (martial uncle), Pak Cheung. Pak Cheung lived outside of Foshan. In 1995, Andreas Hoffman was given a certificate recognizing him as a successor of Jee Shim Wing Chun ("Chi Sim Ving Tsun kung fu from Siu Lum"). Today, Hoffman preserves the art of his teacher and ancestors throughout Europe with a strong organization of over 3000 members.

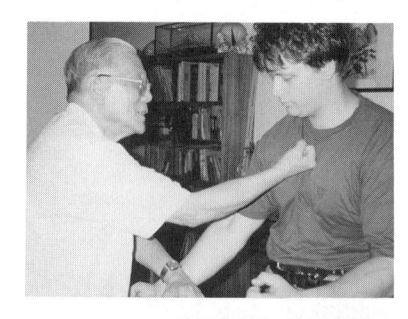

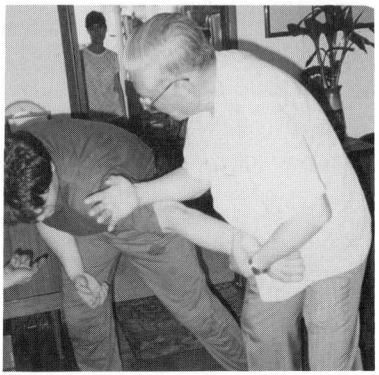

Way Yan demonstrates the finer points of Jee Shim Wing Chun.

BASIC MOVEMENTS

Jee Shim Wing Chun kuen has many observable Siu Lam influences. Another art that bears many similarities to Jee Shim Wing Chun in stance, body structure, and application is Hung ga kuen. Hung ga kuen and Wing Chun kuen are both said to have been derived from the same source, Abbott Jee Shim.

A slogan from Dai Duk Lam: *Ying Yee Lei Fa Shu* (Form, Intention, Principles, Methods, and Art) by Way Yan.

Stances include the *kay lung ma* (astride the dragon stance), *yee jee kim yeung ma* (character two goat clinching stance), *jee ng ma* (forward stance), *sae ping ma* (horse stance), *nu jee ma* (cross stance), and *diu ma* (hanging stance), also known as *ding jee ma* (T-shape stance).

Beginners are drilled in basic training that includes *jin kuen* (arrow fist), a method of straight-line and angular advancing while striking. Jee Shim Wing Chun includes many other fist and palm striking methods, elbow and shoulder maneuvers, kicking, joint locking, and throwing techniques. It is quite different from the other systems of Wing Chun in both content and appearance.

Hand strikes include the horizontal fist, vertical fist, backfist, and a myriad of vertical and horizontal palm strikes. The arm does not extend more than ninety-percent while striking. Jee Shim Wing Chun favors a right leading *diu ma* stance as the preferred fighting position, and slanted body position. A Jee Shim Wing Chun practitioner will not face his opponent squarely, and one is advised to *"Teng nuo yee shun shuok"* (Rise up, jump about, and shift quickly), and *"Bien jing mok yan chi"* (Side and frontal body positions

Andreas Hoffman, Dagmar Hoffman and Way Yan in Hong Kong.

Hoffman, Way Yan and Cheng Kwong pose with the first Muk Yan Jong in Hong Kong.

be done without delay). As in other forms of Wing Chun, there are the standard movements of *tan, bong, fook, gaun,* and *huen,* but they are not as emphasized. Kicks include the *liu yum gerk* (a slanted kick to the groin), *fu mei gerk* (tiger tail kick), *chuen sum gerk* (heart stamping kick), and others. Joint locks include finger, wrist, arm, and leg breaks, and simultaneous body-to-joint breaks and throws. Jee Shim Wing Chun is truly a collection of life saving arts.

FORMS AND TRAINING

The Jee Shim Wing Chun curriculum includes its core empty-hand set *sam bai fut* (three prayers to Buddha), which makes use of footwork in all directions, and teaches body structure and mechanics. *Sam bai fut* is the beginning and end of Jee Shim Wing Chun Kuen. It is said that Way Yan and Chu Chong-Man practiced together at the Dai

Duk Lan for twenty-six years and tried to exhaust the infinite applications of the set's movements. This shows the depth of this important set.

On the whole, the sets of Jee Shim Wing Chun kuen move in all directions and place strong emphasis on footwork. practitioners view their forms as fighting sets, which have actual combat meaning. Another set, *Wing Chun kuen* (Always Spring fist), begins in the static clamping stance but later includes linear footwork and the basic hand forms of the style. Some refer to this set as *Wing Chun sup yat sao* (Wing Chun eleven hands), and it provides an insight into the Jee Shim Wing Chun basics. Also practiced is a set called *jong kuen* (dummy fist), which emphasizes applications from the pole and fist. *Jong kuen* contains seven conceptual hand techniques that are based on the system's pole set. It is believed to be a set passed on from Chu Chung-Man. A set of *muk yan jong* (wooden dummy) maneuvers is also taught, This set is broken down into *tien yan dei* (the trinity of Heaven, earth, and man), and represents applications of the dummy in respect to attacking the opponent's head, torso, and lower body. Interesting is the low squatting postures found toward the end of the set.

The *bai jong* (ready position) of Jee Shim Wing Chun.

Jee Shim Wing Chun wooden dummy training.

The pole is the favored weapon in Jee Shim Wing Chun, and the *luk dim boon gwun* (six-and-a-half-point pole) set is practiced. The seven conceptual keywords of *tai* (raise), *lan* (obstruct), *dim* (point), *kit* (deflect), *got* (cut), and *lou* (leak) are the main points of the pole set. Interestingly, the Jee Shim fist and pole share the same stances and body structure, unlike the other Wing Chun systems where pole and fist are quite different. Moreover, combinations of movements and concepts of the *seung dao* (double knives) are also practiced.

Partner training in Jee Shim Wing Chun includes *chi sao* (sticking hands) and *san sao* (separate techniques). *Chi sao* begins in a double palm up position, and there is no rolling of the hands as in other forms in Wing Chun. This is again practiced in the *diu ma* stance with the right leg leading. *Chi sao* is not a static training, but a free flowing art of feeling and sensitivity. One emphasizes using body structure in all blows, and not just being limited to mere limb strength. *Chi sao* in Jee Shim Wing Chun includes all of the art's striking, joint locking, and throwing techniques

Andreas Hoffman sifu demonstrates a movement from *sam bai fut*.

San sao is taught throughout the curriculum and is explained in the applications of the various sets. Andreas Hoffman explains that Jee Shim Wing Chun is ninety-percent fighting application and ten-percent forms practice. There are no elaborate two-man forms, and applications are flexible.

Hoffman sifu applies a technique from the three prayers to Buddha set.

CONCEPTS AND PRINCIPLES

Many of the concepts and principles of Jee Shim Wing Chun are preserved in oral traditions known as *kuen kuit* (fist sayings) or *ho kuit* (oral sayings). Many of these sayings are identical to the other branches of Wing Chun, thus indicating a common source.

In Jee Shim Wing Chun, the fist is considered the root of the system, containing all the applications. The staff is considered the teacher as it is long and heavy and the stress of applying it causes one to utilize the body structure. The double knives are considered the parents as they teach a student to give birth to many variations.

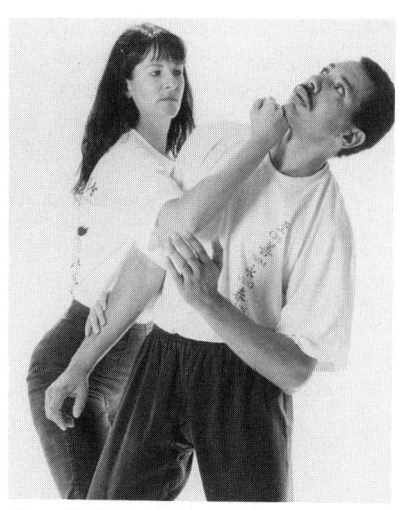

The following five sayings (with translation and explanation) are but examples of the Jee Shim oral traditions:

• *Teng nuo yee shun shuok* (Jump about, and grind quickly). The body positions and footwork must be nimble and quick.
• *Bien jing mok yan chi* (Side and frontal body positions be done without delay). In facing one's opponent, one can change to frontal (square) or side facing (slant body) positions.
• *Lui lao hui sung* (As he comes, flow; as he goes, escort). This common Wing Chun saying refers to the close-quarter fighting range.
• *Lut sao jik chung* (When one has lost control of the hands, rush in like a flood). This refers to close fighting range with an opponent.
• *Sao gerk dui siu, mo jit jiu* (Hands and feet defend accordingly, there are no unstoppable techniques).

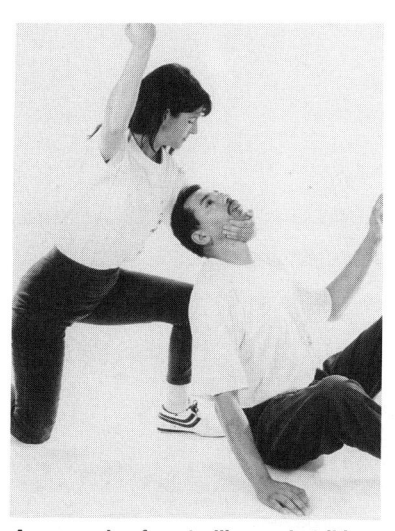

Nava Hoffman demonstrates a simultaneous controlling and striking application.

Four favorable situations for Jee Shim Wing Chun practitioners include *bok* (closing in and butting in combat, to pounce upon, fight), *fook* (to defeat, subdue, and control your opponent), *yao* (to lead the opponent to induce your opponent's reaction), and *lao* (to leak into an opponent's defense).

An example of controlling and striking at the low-line level.

Since Jee Shim Wing Chun kuen came directly out of the Siu Lam temple, and Jee Shim was a *sim si* (Zen master), the art is taught with overtones for reaching enlightenment. As in seated meditation, the active goal of Jee Shim Wing Chun is to reach enlightenment where a student's mind is able to go free, and simply flow with the circumstances. The forms of Jee Shim Wing Chun can be seen as a *hua to* (Zen koan) for the student to solve in order to reach ultimate reality.

CONCLUSION

Jee Shim Wing Chun may provide us with the earliest link as to what was practiced on the Red Boats. The conceptual groundwork and similarity between this system and Siu Lam are evident in stances, fighting tactics, and physical and mental training. Jee Shim Wing Chun is extremely rare now in China and Hong Kong, as it was taught in relative secrecy. It has remained virtually unknown to even Wing Chun practitioners around the world. It is hoped that through the efforts of Way Yan, Cheng Kwong, and Andreas Hoffman, this art will be preserved for generations to come as it is an important legacy of the Wing Chun system and family of martial arts.

Andreas Hoffman in a movement from the *sam bai fut* set.

Chapter 9

OTHER WING CHUN KUEN STYLES

Throughout the history of Wing Chun, many highly skilled individuals have learned the style, mastered it, and passed along their teachings. Each master brought to Wing Chun unique insight, experience, and genius. As a result, over the generations many extraordinary interpretations of Wing Chun have evolved. While the preceding chapters have presented seven of these branches, there remain many others in both China and Southeast Asia.

FUJIAN WING CHUN KUEN

Fujian Wing Chun represents a group of similar styles said to descend from the Fujian Siu Lam Jee (Shaolinsi or Young Forest Temple). Legends hold that Jee Shim taught the martial arts in the Wing Chun Dien (Always Spring Hall) of the temple. Following Siu Lam's destruction, several of his disciples were said to have spread his teachings including Fong Sai-Yuk and Hu Hui-Gan who brought the art to Guangdong.

The basic curriculum includes *fa kuen* (variegated fist), *mui fa baat gwa* (plum blossom eight trigrams), *ping yao kuen* (level smooth boxing), *fut jeung* (Buddha's palm), *baat sik dan da* (eight form single hit), *lien wan kao da* (continuous capture hit), *jong kuen* (dummy boxing), and *luk dim boon gwun* (six-and-a-half-point pole).

HUNG SUEN HAY BAN WING CHUN KUEN

Not to be confused with the Wong family style of a similar name, this variation is said to come from the Red Junk Opera of the modern era. While people such as Leung Jan and Fung Siu-Ching had begun to spread the art beyond the opera decades earlier, it is held that Wing Chun also remained on the Junks, continuing its development and gaining other influences. The art was introduced in the United States by Yeung Fook. Yeung Fook learned it on board the Red Junks while a member of the Opera Company in the early 1900s. Yeung Fook taught his art to David Harris, and is also said to have been an influence on Bruce Lee when Lee moved to the U.S. In England, Leung Kwok-Keung (Liang Guoqiang) teaches a different version of the style.

Yeung Fook's style is said to consist mainly of separate techniques and to have a southern mantis flavor. Leung Kwok-Keung's system has modified and expanded the forms *siu nim tao, chum kiu, biu jee, muk yan jong, luk dim boon gwun* (six-and-a-half-point pole), and *wu dip dao* (butterfly knives). It has also integrated other sets like the footwork intensive *chut lun* (seven wheels), *cheung lung tan yue* (long dragon explores the moon) which includes claws and kicks, and *bak hok tan sui* (white crane explores water) which integrates the movements of the three Wing Chun forms and the wooden dummy. It is also said to include other weapons as well.

MALAYSIAN WING CHUN KUEN

Wing Chun was brought to Malaysia in the 1930s by Yip Kin. Yip Kin was said to have been a practitioner of the "Always Spring" or Hung ga style who later learned some of the Wing-Chun art from his wife and/or father-in-law. His teachers were said to have included So Koi-Ming (a student of Leung Kwai-Lam) and/or Ching Tan-Kin. In the 1930s, Yip Kin moved from Guangdong to Malaysia where he began spreading the style in Kuala Lumpur. Yip Kin passed away in 1968, leaving his Malaysian Wing Chun to his son, Yip Fook-Chok, and students such as Wong Yan-Sang.

Malaysian Wing Chun forms retain the traditional salutation (signifying the overthrow of the Qing and restoration of the Ming) that is commonly seen in southern Chinese martial arts styles such as Hung kuen. The curriculum consists of *siu fa kuen* (small flower fist), *dai fa kuen* (big flower fist), *fook fu kuen* (subdue tiger form), *siu ng ying* (small five animals), *tiet pao jang* (iron elbow), *yum yeung baat gwa gwun* (yin yang eight trigram pole), *muk yan jong* (wooden dummy), *luk dim boon gwun* (six-and-a-half-point pole), *wu dip seung dao* (double butterfly knives), *mui fa cheung* (plum blossom spear), *lao yip seung dao* (willow leaf double knives), *fook fu dai pa* (subdue tiger big trident), *chun chiu dai dao* (big spring autumn knives), and various two-person sets. For sensitivity training, Malaysian Wing Chun uses a more complex form of single sticking hands comprising eight hand motions. These hand movements link linear and circular techniques to teach the basics of dominating the centerline, circumventing the centerline, and losing and regaining the centerline, coupled with pivoting and stepping. In addition there are two types of double sticking hands; the first type works on dominating the inner gate using up and down motions and the second one uses the arms to draw circles while maintaining contact to constantly circle from inner to outer gate back to inner gate.

PIEN SAN WING CHUN KUEN

Pien san (side body) Wing Chun has its roots in the Gulao village teachings of Dr. Leung Jan. Retiring from his pharmacy in Foshan at the age of 73, Leung Jan returned to his native village of Gulao in nearby Heshan. There, he made the acquaintance of his neighbor, Wong Wah-Sum, who seemed intent upon developing the skills of self-defense. Deciding to take on a few students, Leung Jan taught Wong Wah-Sum, Yik Ying, Leung Bak-Cheung, and others until he passed away at the age of 76. The Gulao branch of Wing Chun was taught exclusively to native villagers. Wong Wah-Sum's students included Fung Lim (known as "Fei Lo" Lim or "Fat Man" Lim) and Koo Siu-Lung. Fung Lim was said to have previously spent over a decade and a half practicing Fujian Siu Lam fist and mixed the methods, leading him to develop a fierce approach to Wing Chun. The Fung family, including Fung Lim, Fung Seung-Hoi, and Fung Lim's son, Fung Sang (generally credited as the founder of the side body branch of Gulao Wing Chun), eventually moved to the nearby provincial capitol of Guangzhou. Having learned from his father and from his martial uncle, Koo Siu-Lung, Fung Sang possessed a well-rounded knowledge of the art. Among Fung Sang's students were said to have been Sung Chen and Lee Shing (who may also have studied under Fung Yee-Min and Ng Jung-So, and later in Hong Kong with Yip Man, Lok Yiu, and Jiu Wan). Another student of Fung Lim and Koo Siu-Lung, Lee Ding moved to Canada in the late 1980s where he taught a few students.

The Pien San Wing Chun, like most branches, uses short bridges and narrow stances, primarily the *yee jee kim yeung ma* ("yee" character clamping *yang* stance). It favors a relaxed upper body and agile stances and steps that can move and turn dynamically. It also makes use of the *fong ngan chui* (phoenix eye punch). The style itself is composed of a set of *san sao* (separate techniques) which makes heavy use of *pien san ma* (side body stance) turning, the spear-technique inspired *sam dim boon gwun* (three and a half point pole), and a set of southern *Siu Lam Seung dao* (Shaolin double knives).

VIETNAMESE WING CHUN

Accounts name the founder of Vietnamese Wing Chun (romanized by practitioners as Vinh Xuan), as Ngyen Te-Cong (Yuen Chai-Wan) or sometimes Luong Vu-Te. As there are many parallels in their stories, they may be referring to the same individual (with some accounts having been distorted over time). Stories of Ngyen Te-Cong relate that he was born in 1877 in Foshan and was said to have learned under Leung Jan, alongside Chan Wah-Shun, Yuen Kay-San, and Fung Siu-Ching. In 1936 he moved to Hanoi and founded his first school. He later relocated to Saigon in 1955 where he established a second school. Ngyen Te-Cong passed away in 1960 at the age of 84. Among his students was Nguyen Duy-Hai who was born in 1917. Nguyen learned first in Hanoi in 1954 and later continued in Saigon in 1955. Nguyen Duy-Hai died in 1988, leaving his art to Huinh Ngok-An who brought it to Russia in 1990. Tales of Luong Vu-Te maintain he studied under Chan Wah-Shun alongside Yip Man and others. Born in Foshan, but of Vietnamese origins, Luong was said to have later moved back to Vietnam. He was first said to have taught in North Vietnam and later, when peaceful relations were restored, moved south where he taught a different version of the art before passing away in 1973. Among his students was Bac Quy. Accounts of Yuen Chai-Wan (known as Dao Po Chai, or Pok Face Chai) in Foshan hold he was the elder brother of Yuen Kay-San and studied beside him under Fok Bo-Chuen, a student of opera performer Dai Fa Min Kam and Wong Wah-Bo. Later, the Yuen brothers studied under Fung Siu-Ching (another of Kam's students) at their home in Mulberry Gardens, alongside Ma Jung-Yiu, Au Shi, Lo Hao-Po, and others. In the 1930s, he was invited to teach Wing Chun in Vietnam, at the Nanhai and Shunde Associations by Chinese expatriates.

Vietnamese Wing Chun includes the *siu nim tao* (*tieu luyen dau* or little idea), *siu mui fa* (*tieu mai hao* or little plum flower), *hok ying sao bo* (*hac hinh thu bo* or crane shape hand step), and *hong lung fook fu kuen* (*hang long phuc ho quen* or conquer dragon subdue tiger fist) forms. They also train with the *muk yan jong* (*moc nhan xuan* or wooden dummy), single and double headed *luk dim boon gwun* (*luc diem bau con* or six-and-a-half-point pole), *baat jaam dao* (*bat tram dao* or eight chopping knives), and are said to be famous for their *gim* (sword). *Hei gung* is reportedly very important to the practice of Vietnamese Wing Chun. In addition to the *ng ying hay gung* (*ngu hinh khi cong* or five shape [animal] *qigong*) form, almost three dozen complex exercises are practiced, encompassing roughly fifty-percent of training.

YIU KAI WING CHUN KUEN

Wing Chun spread from Fujian Siu Lam disciple Yim Sei. To avoid arrest, Yim fled Siu Lam to Guangxi with his daughter, Wing-Chun, where he sold tofu for a living. In around 1810, he began teaching the Fujian martial arts to his daughter. Wing-Chun, while washing clothing one day, saw a snake and crane fighting and found inspiration to refine the styles to better suit her own needs. She later married Siu Lam disciple Leung Bok-Chao, who fell in love with her while watching her practice beneath the moon light. Leung Bok-Chao learned the art from his wife and when Yim Sei passed away a short time later, the couple moved to Shangxi. Due to local turmoil, in 1815 they relocated to Guangdong and began teaching "Wing-Chun's" boxing. They soon settled in Zhaoqing where they continued passing on the art. Zhaoqing was a common stop on the Red Junk Opera performers' route. During one of the shows, Leung Bok-Chao and Yim Wing Chun met performers Wong Wah-Bo (who played the martial lead), Leung Yee-Tai (who played the "female" martial lead), Dai Fa Min Kam (who played the painted face role), and Siu Fook (who played the romantic lead). Striking up a friendship, the performers soon became their students. Wong Wah-Bo and Leung Yee-Tai later retired to Foshan where they taught their skills to the son of a pharmacist named Leung Jan. Dr. Leung Jan spread the art throughout Foshan. His most renowned student was Chan Wah-Shun who taught Wing Chun to Ng Jung-So and others. Ng Jung-So passed his art along to his son, Ng Yat-Fei, and to students Fok Joy and Yiu Choi. (some accounts suggest Yiu Choi also received lessons from Chan Wah-Shun). Yiu Choi handed the art on to his son, Yiu Kai (who some relate also received training under Ng Jung-So). Yiu Kai taught Wing Chun in Foshan for decades to students such as Leung Keung, Tang Wai-Po, and others.

Yiu Kai Wing Chun follows the key concepts of *tan* (spread-out), *fook* (subdue), *bong* (wing), and the cardinal principle *"lui lao hui soong, lut sao jik chung"* (keep what comes, send off what goes, charge straight when the hand is free).

OTHER BRANCHES

There remain yet other branches of the Wing Chun art that are not as widely known. Go Lo Chung of the Red Junk Opera passed along his version of Wing Chun to his son-in-law, Yin Lee-Cheung. Leung Jan was said to have taught many students, including Lai Yeung-Yin, also known as Lai Ying. Lai Yeung-Yin passed his art along to Wong Jing who later practiced alongside Sum Nung under Yuen Kay-San. Wong Jing taught few people, among them was said to be Mai Gai Wong (Rice Machine Wong) who was also said to have learned a little from several other instructors and gained a large following in the region. Fung Siu-Ching's student, Leung Yan taught his brother, Leung Jik, and together they passed along Wing Chun in Foshan.

Conclusion

The previous chapters have presented numerous differing views on the genesis and evolution of the Wing Chun style. These histories provide many intriguing scenarios but leave many unanswered questions. What then are the personal conclusions of the authors? It very difficult to say with any certainty who created and developed the Wing Chun style. Presented here, however, are the authors' own opinions and speculations as broken down into five critical stages. While conclusions almost inevitably create controversy, it is hoped that our Wing Chun brothers will consider our thoughts with open minds and generous hearts.

STAGE 1, PREDECESSORS OF WING CHUN

Wing Chun's early history exists more in fiction than in fact. Over the centuries, many popular folk-tales have sprung up, each dramatic and exciting in its own right, which seek to explain the origin of this great group of styles. Throughout the myriad legends, many individuals have come to be linked in one way or another with the founding of the style. These people and their connections to Wing Chun's genesis, whether real, based on reality, or woven from the fabric of age-old stories, have come to be an important part of Wing Chun's richly textured past.

Due to the revolutionary activities of the time martial artists sometimes hid behind nicknames, stage names and, in some cases (due to modesty or marketing), linked their arts and innovations to fictitious archetypal characters or the names of real but unconnected historical figures. In fact, in ancient China it was not uncommon to create an art and then attribute it to a famous ancestor or mythical founder so that the art would look more valid.

Rather than "new and improved," the Chinese tended to place more value in arts they perceived as ancient and traditional.

The historical accounts of Pan Nam Wing Chun place the beginning of the art which would become Wing Chun in the mid-1670s with the founding of the Tien Dei Wui (Tian Di Hui or Heaven and Earth Society) anti-Qing revolutionary movement. This can perhaps be seen as the catalyst which would ultimately lead to the development of Wing Chun. In the 1640s, when the Manchurians invaded China, they overthrew the Ming Dynasty of the Han nation and established the Qing Dynasty. The Siu Lam Jee (Shaolinsi or Young Forest Temples) gave shelter to the Ming loyalists and revolutionary movements quickly sprang up around, and within, the temples. In some cases, the monks themselves may have been involved while in others the revolutionaries took on the names and habits of the monks to disguise their true purposes. During this time, martial arts development turned to techniques that could be learned quickly and used effectively to counter the classical arts employed by the Manchurians. This could be the ancient root of the core san sao (separate techniques) which would later filtered down to the Guangdong Hung Suen Hay Ban (Cantonese Red Junk Opera Company).

It is said that the main Siu Lum temple was in Songshan, Henan. Oral accounts suggest that there were also temples in Fujian, Jiangxi, Guangdong, among other locations. This has led to some confusion as to which temple Wing Chun legends are associated with.

Since Wing Chun, in all its myriad forms, resembles the martial arts of Fujian and Guangdong far more then it does the northern styles, it is likely that if a strong Shaolin connection truly exists, it is to be found in the Fujian temple. It should be noted, however, that while the Henan temple, rebuilt several times over the millennium still exists today, there is no Fujian Shaolin or remnants to support the fact that it ever existed. Perhaps this fits with the old legends of Shaolin being laid to waste by the Manchurians, leading to the spread of the ancestors of Wing Chun. Conversely, perhaps the existence of the temple is nothing more then a folk story and Wing Chun's origins lie instead in the simple villages of these regions.

While Wing Chun is only thought to have acquired its name much later (during the early 1800s), the roots of the name may well date back to this period. There are many different stories that suggest how the Wing Chun style got its name. Some have speculated that the name Wing Chun was used to honor and remember the Wing Chun Tong (Always Spring Hall) of the Siu Lum Temple where the fabled Jee Shim taught the martial arts (since this hall does not exist in the Henan Temple, it may have been in the legendary Fujian Shaolin temple). Some hold that the art was practiced in Yongchun (Wing Chun or Always Spring) county in Fujian province and was hence named Yongchunquan (the boxing art of Yongchun county). Pan Nam Wing Chun relates that the name Always Spring was formed from the name of revolutionary leader Chan Wing-Wah and a combination of the characters *yat* (sun), *tai* (great), and *tin* (heaven), referring to the Ming dynasty and Heaven and Earth Rebellion. One very popular tale holds simply that it was named in honor of its fabled founder, Yim Wing-Chun. One of the more interesting stories comes from the Pao Fa Lien style which states that the name is a reduction of the revolutionary slogan: *"Wing yun chi jee; mo mong Hon juk; Dai day wui chun"* (Always speak with determination; Don't forget the Han nation; Again will return spring).

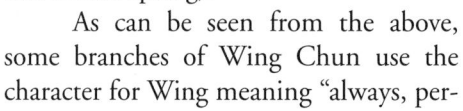

As can be seen from the above, some branches of Wing Chun use the character for Wing meaning "always, perpetual, everlasting," while others use the meaning "to recite, to sing, to chant." Some accounts hold that the former character was changed to the latter in attempts to further obscure its anti-Qing meaning. It is possible, however, that since that both characters sound similar and were passed along verbally, sometimes the version used may have changed back and forth from generation to generation.

We may never know the true origin of the name, but it should be noted that during the Qing dynasty, the name Wing Chun (Always Spring version), with its deep revolutionary meaning, had been used by many different styles from the Fujian area. This included the ancestor of Hung ga kuen (wing chun kuen) and white crane (wing chun bak hok kuen). These systems may or may not have shared a common origin but they shared a common purpose—to overthrow the Qing and restore the Ming. While the other styles had more unique names by which they later attained fame (and became more commonly known), the unique fighting methods of the Hung Suen had no other name, which may be why the Wing Chun name stuck.

The character for wing meaning "always, perpetual, everlasting."

The character for wing meaning "to recite, to sing, to chant."

STAGE 2, FOUNDERS OF WING CHUN

We believe that the seeds of what has become Wing Chun were sown on the Red Junks by Cheung Ng (Zhang Wu), known as Tan Sao Ng for his peerless skill with the technique. He is mentioned in both the historical accounts of the Guangdong opera, written by authors such as Mok Siu-Ha and Man Yiu, and the transmissions of the Pan Nam and Hung Suen Wing Chun styles.

It is unanimously stated that Cheung Ng settled in Foshan, Guangdong where he organized the Red Junk Opera, founding the Hung Fa Wui Goon (Red Flower Union), and taught his skills to the members of the company.

Since the Red Junks gave birth to the early forms of Wing Chun, it is reasonable to assume that Cheung Ng's material had at least some influence on the genesis of the style. In addition, Cheung's nickname, Tan Sao, is the name of one of the principle techniques of Wing Chun kuen. Whether Cheung's art was an orthodox northern system or a revolutionary collection of separate techniques and concepts is unknown. In either case, it probably did not greatly resemble the Wing Chun we see today. What then did Cheung Ng's martial arts resemble?

Opera accounts state simply that Cheung Ng of Wu Pak was highly skilled in both northern opera and in the techniques of Siu Lam. Both Hung Suen and Pan Nam Wing Chun trace Cheung Ng's art back to a twenty-second generation Siu Lam disciple known by the Buddhist name Yat Chum ("Speck of dust"). Hung Suen Wing Chun states simply that she was a master of a special form of Siu Lam. Pan Nam's accounts suggest that Cheung knew a blend of Northern styles including tai gik (taiji or great ultimate), tong long (tanglang or preying mantis), ying jow (yingzhao or eagle claw), and gum gang jeung (jingangzhang or diamond palms). Whereas the Pan Nam style may have movements that suggest such an origin, in this respect it is unique among the Wing Chun branches. On examination, tai gik kuen was an art undergoing parallel development at this time in Chenjiagou in Henan province and really unavailable to outsiders until Yang Luchan brought it to Beijing in the early 1800s. Therefore it is highly unlikely that taijiquan could be part of the Wing Chun kuen of the early to mid 1700s. In regard to tong long, while Wing Chun is very similar to southern mantis (in body structure, stance, and techniques), it is not close to northern mantis at all. Ying jow is a famous northern style (with variations in Shandong and Southern China). Again, only Pan Nam Wing Chun has any similarity to a southern version of ying jow with it's three-finger claw grip. Lastly, gum gang jeung is a famous training method for palm techniques in the Shaolin. Wing Chun kuen, while using a great number of palm techniques, does not make use this term to describe them. Without further information, it is difficult to see how Wing Chun is composed of these arts.

A classic saying relates that "Nan quan bei tui" ("The south punches, the north kicks). In general, northern styles stress more diverse and dynamic kicks and their sets typically go from left to right in a straight line. Southern sets, by contrast, typically move in all directions and place their emphasis on handwork. A look at the techniques of Wing Chun forms would indicate they are primarily of southern descent. Yet, forms such as Chum Kiu and Biu Jee are typically done in a straight line from left to right, which may reaffirm a northern influence. Perhaps Cheung Ng did bring northern styles, along with the opera sets (which typically made use of the bold and open movements of northern boxing) and this led to the influence in choreography rather then actual stylistic flavor.

Oral transmissions of both Pan Nam Wing Chun and Hung Suen Wing Chun relate that Cheung Ng personally taught his system to Wong Wah-Bo, Leung Yee-Tai, Dai Fa Min Kam, and others. Pan Nam suggests this occurred in the early- to mid-1800s while Hung Suen indicates the early to mid-1700s. Since the histories of the opera state that Cheung Ng only arrived in Foshan sometime between the early-1720s and mid-1730s (decades before the fabled destruction of both the Henan and Fujian Shaolin temples), it is doubtful he could have lived long enough to have given them personal instruction. Likewise, as Wong, Leung, Kam, and the other opera members involved with Wing Chun were active in the mid-1800s, it is unlikely they could have lived early enough for direct transmission. In all probability, there were a few generations in between the two periods, during which time Wing Chun evolved on the Junks. Perhaps in those few generations, the missing names of inheritors are those preserved in the accounts of the other traditions.

People said to have taught the martial arts to the Red Junk performers (or to their ancestors) include the fabled ng jo (wuzu or five elders) such as Jee Shim Sim Si (Jee Shim Chan Buddhist Teacher) and Ng Mui Si Tai (Five Plums Nun). Links between the Five elders and the Red Junks have included Miu Shun, Miu Tsui-Fa, Fung Sai-Yuk, Yim Yee, Yim Wing-Chun, and Leung Bok-Chao. Whether these characters are fictional archetypes of Southern fist traditions or real people is not entirely clear. Since these characters are popular in folk novels and have been romanticized in radio stories, newspaper articles, television series, videotape series, and movies, they are well-known throughout southern China. They have become so much a part of the culture that, in some circles, denying their existence is considered blasphemous.

These stories were often set in southern China during the Qing dynasty when the Manchurians treated the Southern Chinese with great cruelty. Heroes strive to overthrow them and to give the people hope may have been a folklore necessity. In these times, if one's art was connected to these five quasi-deities, it would be considered excellent and unsurpassed, lending it great credibility. Since so many connections to the various famous folk heroes occurred in the history of Wing Chun, it is most likely that the art's history became distorted with the addition of these fables.

Stories about the five elders' activities ranged from the fairly reasonable to the outrageously absurd. Some may suggest that tales of the five elders are found in so many different styles and accounts, that there must be some kernel of truth to them. In fact, many who have written and continue to write stories about the origins of southern Chinese martial arts time and again refer to the fables of the "five elders." It should be noted, however, that during the Qing dynasty, martial art pulp novels (romanticized soap opera-like stories) were already in circulation and some, like *Wan Nian Qing* (Ten Thousand Years Green) contained highly dramatized accounts of the five elders turning on, and eventually killing, each other. As these stories have, over the generations, become accepted history in several styles, it is not hard to imagine that they may be the source of the similar accounts, rather then referring to an actual group of "five elders."

Of the five elders, two in particular are very closely tied to the fables of Wing Chun. Jee Shim is linked to many southern martial arts including the famous five major family systems of southern China (Hung, Lao, Choy, Lee, and Mok). Following his departure from Siu Lam, he reportedly wandered the country looking for students to aid in the resistance. Many accounts have him eventually joining the Red Junk troupes and introducing them to the Wing Chun (Always Spring) style and the luk dim boon gwun (six-and-a-half-point pole). It is uncertain whether Jee Shim himself taught Hung Suen members Wong Wah-Bo, Leung Yee-Tai, Dai Fa Min Kam, and others directly (as many legends suggest), or if the art(s) attributed to him simply came down to the Red Junks through the generations. It is interesting to note that some versions of the "Always Spring" style and Hung ga kuen share similar characteristics, and both name Jee Shim as their source.

In legend, Ng Mui is named as an inheritor of Siu Lam kuen (Young Forest boxing), Wudangquan (Wudang boxing), and/or Ngok ga kuen (Yuejiaquan or Ngok family boxing), and/or as the founder of Wing Chun kuen (Wing-Chun's boxing), Ng Mui pai (Wu Mei pai or Ng Mui's style), lung ying mor kiu (dragon shape rubbing bridges), bak hok kuen (white crane boxing), ng ying hung kuen (five shape hung boxing). One tale also names her as the daughter of a Ming general. A favorite folk hero and revolutionary cover story, she is also linked to many different places, among them Mo Dong San (Wudangshan) in Hebei, Siu Lum Jee (Shaolinsi) in Henan or Fujian, Ngo Mei San (Emeishan) in Sichuan, Bak Hok Jee (Baihesi) in Yunnan or Sichuan, as well as various locations in Guangxi, and Guangdong.

There are many, many fables about Ng Mui. These stories, long favored by the pulp novelists, provide few real explanations and leave many questions unanswered. Sophisticated martial art development is seldom, if ever, the product of a few moments of inspiration derived from watching animals fight, or even a few months of speedy teaching, but of years and generations of careful refinement. To think that a talented martial artist can be inspired by a snake and crane fighting and develop a completely new martial arts system is almost incomprehensible. Time and again, however, the fable of Ng Mui creating the Wing Chun system is told to new, naive students by their sifu as if they were divine facts carved in stone. In our opinions, it is doubtful that any of these stories are real and that Ng Mui is more then likely connected to Wing Chun only in fable. Although such tales can be romantic and inspirational, and certainly have their place in the rich culture of Wing Chun, it is important to clearly distinguish them from historical fact.

Perhaps the name "Ng Mui," similar to "Cheung Ng" (in that the character "five" is present in both their names) provides the convenience of tacking on a famous character to the origin of Wing Chun to help popularize the art and cover the various revolutionaries.

Miu Tsui-Fa, daughter of elder Miu Hin, and sometime student of Ng Mui, is occasionally mentioned as having taught the double knives to Yim Yee and/or Yim Wing-Chun. As the Wing Chun knife methods are almost indistinguishable from the fist fighting methods, it is very difficult to believe that they were added in from an external source (unless the legends describe Miu Tsui-Fa giving an actual pair of knives to the fabled Yim Wing-Chun).

Fong Sai-Yuk, son of Miu Tsui-Fa, was another larger-than-life martial arts folk hero. Reportedly bathed in *dit da jow* (falling and hitting wine; a type of herbal medicine) since birth to make him practically invulnerable, he was the subject of numerous pulp novels (and in more recent times, movies). In fables of Fujian Wing Chun, Fong Sai-Yuk was said to have been a disciple of Jee Shim alongside Hung Hay-

Goon, and was reputed to be an expert in many types of martial arts, including Fujian Wing Chun which it is claimed he later spread. Due again to a lack of supporting material and the Chinese martial penchant for linking styles to famous folk personalities, we think it is doubtful a strong connection exists between Fong and what is commonly considered to be the major Wing Chun branches.

Yim Yee, also called by the name Yim Sei or by the nickname Yee Gung (Grandfather Yee), is sometimes cast only as the father of Yim Wing-Chun while other tales give him a much more important role. One fable holds that he was a Siu Lam disciple who later received training from a Guangxi monk named Miu Shun. Mui Shun was said to have been a student of Ng Mui who mixed the nun's white crane boxing with his own style to create a new system. One interesting account suggests that in the late 1700s Yim Yee was a revolutionary connected to both the Fujian temple, and the Hung Mun Society's militant Hung Gwun (Red Pole) sect. A master of such advanced systems as Wing Chun bak hok kuen (Always Spring white crane boxing), sae ying kuen (snake shape boxing), and others, one story relates that it was Yim Yee himself who created Wing Chun. Distilling his knowledge, he was said to have named the style in honor of the place in which he lived, Yongchun (Wing Chun) County, Fujian. Most accounts, however, relate that Yim Yee fled Fujian with his daughter to avoid arrest at the hands of the Qing and sold tofu for a living in either Guangxi or Yunnan. As Guangxi borders on both Fujian and Guangdong, it is perhaps a more likely transitional location for the art.

Yim Wing-Chun is another famous subject of pulp novels and modern movies. Many legends exist of her learning Wing Chun from Ng Mui, and one even relates that it was she and not her famed mistress who witnessed the fight between the snake and the crane. The stories of Yim Wing Chun having to learn martial arts for revenge or to spurn a ruffian's harassment and advances lend a great romantic twist to the story of Wing Chun. It has, however, led to the mistaken impression that Wing Chun kuen can be mastered in a very short time (although Wing Chun kuen may be learned in a relatively short time, years of practice are required to truly master it).

Another version of this story suggests that in the early 1800s, Yim Wing-Chun learned snake and crane shape boxing, and possibly other Fujian methods, from her father, Yim Yee, and refined them to better suit her own body structure. These stories, involving the combination of Wing Chun white crane boxing with snake shape boxing does provide some intriguing possibilities. A comparison of modern Wing Chun kuen with Fujian Wing Chun bak hok kuen and sae ying kuen reveals some strong similarities. Perhaps there is a grain of truth in these stories and Wing Chun could be a combination of both of these arts. It is not impossible to think that the folkstory of a snake and crane fighting originated with the actual blending of snake and crane boxing.

The Hung Suen style, by contrast, suggests that the name Yim Wing-Chun was merely an expansion of the Wing Chun revolutionary motto, adding the character Yim (meaning, "protect"). This lends doubt to whether or not Yim Wing-Chun was, in fact, a real person. Perhaps the name was again a revolutionary cover hiding the actual person behind these events.

Around 1810, Yim Wing-Chun was said to have encountered and later married Leung Bok-Chao. Many different backgrounds have been given for Leung, including a Choy ga or Hung ga disciple from Zhaoqing, a former Siu Lam disciple from Jiangxi or Henan, a salt merchant, or a performer with the Red Junk Opera. Most tales state that sometime around 1815 or 1820, Leung journeyed to Guangdong and taught his wife's art to Wong Wah-Bo, Leung Yee-Tai, Dai Fa Min Kam, and other members of the Red Junk. Accounts of the Yip Man style mentioned a man by the name of Leung Lan-Kwai (sometimes said to have been an opera performer, other times an osteopath or wealthy scholar) as the bridge between Leung Bok-Chao and the Red Junk members. All other versions exclude him entirely, or mention him only in passing as a classmate of the other performers.

It is interesting to note that almost exact parallels exist between folk stories of the Wing Chun and Always Spring White Crane styles. Both relay the tale of Ng Mui gaining inspiration to invent their art from witnessing a battle between a snake and a crane. Both have accounts of a father (Yim Sei and Fong Jong respectively) teaching the Fujian Shaolin arts to his daughter (Yim Wing-Chun and Fong Chut-Leung) who then taught their husbands (Leung Bok-Chao and Chung Sei) who later spread the arts. Lastly, both have stories mentioning their being named after Yongchun, Fujian. Due to the similarities, it is possible that these individuals are all just different incarnations of the same archetypal characters, used to disguise the real revolutionaries involved in the arts.

What is also confusing is that in some stories Ng Mui's student was not named Fong Chut-Leung, but rather Fong Wing-Chun. Fong Wing-Chun later became the wife of Hung Hay-Goon. Hung allegedly combined his Siu Lam tiger fist art learned from Jee Shim and his wife's white crane style to give birth to Hung ga fu hok pai (Hung family tiger crane style). Is this Cantonese version of Fong Wing-Chun actually a bastardization of the story of Fong Chut-Leung (Fang

Qiniang), the actual creator of Fujian Bak Hok kuen (White Crane boxing)? One outlandish account even suggested that Hung Hay-Goon later changed his name to Leung Bok-Chao and went to hide on the Red Junks. The Fujian white crane style and history is so far reaching that it has even spread to Okinawa in the form of hakutsura kenpo (Japanese: white crane fist methods). In fact, the Kuen Po (Fist Register book) of the white crane style, *Wu Pei Chi* (*Bubishi* in Japanese), is revered there by Okinawan karateka. Guangdong is a lot closer to Fujian than Okinawa and the tales of white crane boxing more than likely found their way to Guangdong as well.

One must wonder why the names Fong Wing-Chun and Yim Wing-Chun are so similar, and why all these stories have so many parallels. Some have suggested that they all involved the same people. Again, the authors believe the fables of the five elders and their disciples are just that—fables based, perhaps, on a grain of truth, which have been interwoven into the histories of many southern styles over the years.

STAGE 3, RED JUNK ANCESTORS OF WING CHUN

Beyond the Wing Chun Kuen of early fables, many remarkable masters have inherited the art and passed it on to new generations. Each, doubtless, brought to the style their own unique genius and experience, and thus they form the link between the Wing Chun of legend and the Wing Chun practiced in the world today.

Almost without exception, the history of Wing Chun inevitably brings us back to the Red Junks of the mid-1800s. The second stage of the arts development, it is also the first period to which we can reliably trace back the style.

Since the Red Junk Opera Companies could move around with relative ease and often wore heavy make-up that could disguise their appearances, they were an ideal place to seek refuge, and hence became a hot bed of revolutionary activity.

The most commonly named members of the Red Junk who had knowledge of Wing Chun are Wong Wah-Bo, Leung Yee-Tai, Dai Fa Min Kam, and Gao Lo Chung. Each is named in many different accounts and by several different branches. Several accounts also mention a performer by the given name of Fook who played the role of Siu-sang. Practitioners of Pan Nam Wing Chun call him Lai Fook-Shun, while practitioners of Hung Suen Wing Chun relate he was Hung Fook; others have stated he was Siu Fook (Little Fook). While it is possible they may all be referring to different individuals, the similar names, identical parts, and the fact that there are never two Fook's who played Siu-sang mentioned in the same account, give a strong indication that they are all referring to the same individual.

It should also be noted that at first glance the Pao Fa Lien Wing Chun tales about Dai Dong Fung (Great East Wind) may appear distinct from the accounts of Wing Chun spreading from the Red Junks. There are, however, a few tales that suggest Dai Dong Fung spent time aboard the Red Junks and learned the Wing Chun of Leung Bok-Chao, blending it with his previous Siu Lam knowledge. Another version holds that he was a fellow Red Junk performer and the Siu Lam monk tale was a revolutionary cover story, or archetypal account. An alternate story places the origin of Pao Fa Lien with a Hung ga kuen practitioner name Lee Ying who later blended his art with Wing Chun. In either case, these stories may account for both the similarities and differences seen in the Pao Fa Lien style.

The Red Junk members knew a vast and diverse amount of martial arts, both for performance and for fighting. As opera performers, Wong Wah-Bo, Leung Yee-Tai, "Dai Fa Min" Kam and others needed extensive knowledge of visually dynamic boxing and weapon techniques. This is probably where the northern martial arts and the more crowd-pleasing southern styles were utilized. As revolutionaries, the Red Junk members needed martial arts primarily intended for close-range self-defense and the assassination of Qing officials on the boats and in the narrow rooms and alleys of southern China. This is most likely why the Wing Chun style evolved as it did.

The Gu Lao branch records that initially Wing Chun consisted only of separate hand techniques practiced on a wooden dummy, with a partner, and with double knives. It is likely that the opera performers explored and refined all of their knowledge, distilling the core movements of the arts and linking them together. This is probably when the forms seen in most of Wing Chun, such as *siu nim/lin tao* (little idea/first training), *chum kiu* (seeking/sinking bridge), and *biu jee* (darting fingers) were choreographed. The six-and-a-half-point pole techniques were also integrated at this point, becoming a fundamental weapon alongside the double knives and possibly the *fei biu* (flying darts).

The three major boxing forms are fairly consistent in organization throughout the various styles. The wooden dummy, pole, and knife techniques, by contrast, all share similar techniques but are choreographed very differently from branch to branch. This may suggest that while the boxing forms were formalized early on during the Red Junk period, dummy, pole, and knife techniques remained only loosely grouped, without choreographed routines until much later.

Since each opera performer possessed a wide and varied knowledge of the martial arts, each would later pass along a slightly different version of Wing Chun kuen and over the generations, through natural evolutionary changes, personal taste, innovation, and experience, the different branches of Wing Chun kuen would develop.

Thus, since all Wing Chun schools come from the same source, although they diversified almost immediately, arguments over which branch has preserved the authentic, orthodox, traditional method have become moot. All have, and none have.

STAGE 4, DISSEMINATORS OF WING CHUN

The next great stage of Wing Chun development probably began in the mid- to late-1800s as the art moved off the Red Junks and expanded into several of the local villages along their route (including Zhaoqing, Foshan, and Guangzhou). Many of the individuals who learned during this period became renowned for their fighting skills and the art of Wing Chun, for the first time, began to become known and highly respected outside its own tight family.

While a few practitioners of the period were rumored to have carried on the anti-Qing activities, others were professionals who used the style for protecting villages and capturing criminals, and still others used the art for self-defense and in challenge matches with practitioners of other systems. Almost all won great fame for their talents. During this period, Wing Chun likely grew from strict revolutionary defense and assassination to a more well-rounded and tested martial art.

As the Red Junk performers took leave or retired from the Opera in the latter half of the nineteenth century, they passed along their knowledge to Dr. Leung Jan, Fung Siu-Ching, Fok Bo-Chuen, Cao Desheng (Cho Dak-On), Lok Lan-Gong, Cheung Gung, and others. Leung Jan, the student of Wong Wah-Bo and Leung Yee-Tai, is credited with refining Wing Chun and helping to spread the art in Foshan. Cheung Gung, the student of fellow revolutionary "Hung Gan" Biu, kept the art in the family for several generations, teaching his grand-nephew Wong Ting. Both Fok Bo-Chuen and Lok Lan-Gong learned "Dai Fa Min" Kam's art in Foshan and passed it on to only a few select students. Fung Siu-Ching, another disciple of Dai Fa Min Kam, taught many students who expanded Wing Chun throughout Guangdong and into Thailand, Malaysia, Vietnam, and other parts of Southeast Asia. Verbal accounts mentioned that fourteen Wing Chun masters came to Malaysia over the decades. Only two, Cao Desheng's students Cao Dean (Cho Dak-On) and Yip Kin were known to have publicly opened schools.

Both Leung Jan and Fok Bo-Chuen were said to have learned in part from Wong Wah-Bo. This may, along with other factors, account for the great similarity in body structure between what later became the smaller framed, more compact Yuen Kay-San and Yip Man styles of Wing Chun.

Differences in other branches, such as the larger framed and more expansive Pao Fa Lien, Nanyang, Malaysian, and similar Wing Chun systems, probably arise from their integration and preservation of Always Spring and/or Hung ga kuen methods. Shared ancestral elements may have allowed for the easy and effective integration of the differing elements, leading to very well rounded systems.

A third category that developed during this period were the systems composed entirely of separate techniques (no choreographed long forms). Leung Jan, late in life, was said to have taught a forty points system in his native Gu Lao village. Several of Fung Siu-Ching's students also came away with sets of separate techniques such as the twelve forms and eight form single hitting. Since these styles bear some strong similarities, and make use of antique names such as big-taming-tiger and white-crane-catches-the-fox, it is possible they come from the same ancestral set of separate techniques practiced on the Red Junks.

STAGE 5, DEVELOPERS OF WING CHUN

Although Wing Chun made great strides forward and firmly established itself in many places, it is still likely that the modern, refined systems we see in Yip Man, Yuen Kay-San, and other branches were not yet fully developed. From whence did these versions come then? Probably from Yuen Kay-San, Yip Man, and their peers.

Yuen Kay-San learned his forms from Fok Bo-Chuen and his advanced application from Fung Siu-Ching. Following his lessons, Yuen spent years combining his knowledge and refining his art. He was said to have been the first to begin the systematic recording of Wing Chun's modern principles in works such as the twelve methods, the important rhymed formulae, among others.

It should be noted that there have been some conflicting accounts over the years as to who taught Yuen Kay-San. Differing stories have also named him as the student of Leung Jan, Chan Wah-Shun, and Ng Jung-So. This was said to have arisen as Yuen seldom, if ever, mentioned his teachers' names to outsiders. When the authors of the Wing Chun pulp novels that began to circulate from the 1930s attempted to link him, they did so in whatever manner they could. Thus, since Yuen was friendly with some of the above-mentioned Wing Chun practitioners, his lineage became meshed with theirs. Lacking better accounts, many simply came to consider these pulp novels as accurate. Since then, however, the matching accounts of Yuen's students, family, and some of the authors themselves (such as Au Soy-Jee who attempted to correct many inaccuracies in a later work not published at Yuen's own request), have helped clarify the history.

Yip Man received his initial training from Chan Wah-Shun, Leung Jan's prized student. When the old moneychanger retired, Yip Man continued his lessons with Ng Jung-So, one of Chan's most talented disciple. He was also said to have spent much time practicing with his seniors and friends, developing a great level of skill.

There are also a few conflicting accounts of Yip Man's early years. Older versions have stated that Yip Man was born in the mid- to late-1800s (from 1895 to 1898) and began learning from Chan Wah-Shun at around the age of thirteen. In more recent years, it has been said that he was born in 1893 and began learning at the age of nine, or even earlier. Comparing these dates to those of Yip Man's immediate senior classmate, Lai Hip-Chi, we find that Lai was said to have been born in 1898 and to have begun studying under Chan at the age of thirteen. This may suggest that the older dates are more accurate. Some accounts maintain Yip Man went to Hong Kong as a teenager and learned advanced application from Leung Bik, son of Leung Jan. Recently, some of Yip Man's students and descendents have come forward to say that this was merely a story created by Lee Man of the Restaurant Workers Union to help increase interest for the style in Hong Kong. It should be noted that Yip Man himself did not mention Leung Bik in his own writings on Wing Chun history, and he is not mentioned in lineages inside China or in some of the pulp fiction novels (which would have loved such a dramatic story) written about Wing Chun and Yip Man. It is thus impossible to say these stories are certain. What is certain, however, is that Yip Man reached a very advanced level of skill in Wing Chun.

Most of the high-level practitioners of this period were the sons of wealthy merchants, which meant they could both afford the high tuition fees Wing Chun masters commanded and could also spend most of their time practicing (since they didn't need to work for a living). It was said that students of several branches met together in the smokehouses to practice application and discuss ideas, Yip Man and Yuen Kay-San included.

Yip Man, initially, did not take any students in Foshan. Yuen Kay-San, by contrast, adopted a young disciple named Sum Nung in the 1930s. Sum had previously learned Wing Chun *san sao* (fighting techniques) from a man named Cheung Bo. Under Yuen's guidance, Sum Nung continued to develop the system.

Through their efforts, Wing Chun's forms were further refined, and its concepts brought fully into the modern scientific period. During that time, they reportedly practiced chi sao extensively, bringing a whole new level of advancement to the drill. It is interesting to note that both the Yuen Kay-San/Sum Nung and Yip Man styles make use of a similar *poon sao/luk sao* (rolling arm) platforms for chi sao. Other lines do not seem to utilize this, instead making use of methods closer to choreographed two-man forms, Tai Ji's tui sao (tuishou or push hands), or entirely different methods. It is not impossible to imagine that what is now considered sticking arms comes from the refinements of Yuen Kay-San and his student Sum Nung as well as Yip Man, and perhaps a few others in their circle.

Sum Nung moved to Guangzhou in the 1940s. There he integrated the separate techniques of Cheung Bo into his training curriculum and wooden dummy set. He continued his development of the style, refining it over the years as he began to accept his own students.

While Yip Man did teach a few students in Foshan, his greatest efforts were made when he moved to Hong Kong in 1949. There he further refined his system, reorganizing and revising his forms (varying them from time to time and student to student). Yip Man's very individualistic teaching method lead to him producing very talented disciples, however, it also lead to a system with different branches and varying opinions of what Yip Man taught.

During the latter part of this period, as Wing Chun began to be taught more publicly and to more students, it is likely that the dummy, pole, and knife methods began to be set into routines. Since the branches were already separated at this point, this probably accounts for the similarity in general techniques but the differences in choreography.

Following Yip Man's death, petty politics, scandal, and a scramble for power amongst his various students lead to strong fragmentation within the art. It is hoped that with the availability of more factual information and the goodwill and sincere efforts of the individuals involved, the art will be brought closer together again.

FINAL THOUGHTS

Although these are our current thoughts based on our shared research and speculation, we will never really know the truth (short of going back in time to the misty past of olden China). Even with the separation of only a few short generations we are already facing vast holes in some instances either through incomplete, inconsistent, fictionalized, or lost accounts. Hopefully the publication of *Complete Wing Chun* will inspire others to come forward and share their information before more knowledge is lost to the passage of time. It is sincerely hoped that this work will not be misused to merely create more believable "ancient mythical marketing slants" for newly formed "lost branches" of Wing Chun kuen.

詠春拳派系統表

The Wing Chun Kuen Family Tree

Founders

- Leung Yee-Tai ─── Leung Jan
  - Wong Wah-Sum
  - Leung Bak-Cheung
  - Yik Ying
  - Others (Gulao)
  - Leung Chun
  - Leung Bik
  - Lai Yeung-Yin
  - "Muk Yan" Wah
  - Lo Kwai
  - Chan Kwai
  - Leung Kai
  - Fung Wah
  - Lao Man-Kay
  - Chan Wah-Shun
  - Ho Han-Lui
  - Tse Biu
  - Others (Foshan)

- Wong Wah-Bo
  - Leung Jan
  - Fok Bo-Chuen

- "Fa Jee" Ming

- Leung Lan-Kwai

- "Gao Lo" Chung ─── Yin Li-Cheung

- "Do Ngan" Shun

- Lai Fook-Shun ─── Fung Siu-Ching
  - Yuen Chai-Wan
  - Yuen Kay-San
  - Leung Yan
  - Fung Ting
  - Dong Jit
  - Lo Hao-Po
  - Dong Suen
  - Lo Ying-Nam
  - Lo Gai-Dong
  - Ma Jung-Yiu
  - Au Si
  - Others…

- Sun Fook-Chun

- "Dai Fa Min" Kam ─── Fok Bo-Chuen
  - Yuen Kay-San
  - Yuen Chai-Wan

- Lo Man-Gong
  - Cho Dak-Sang
    - Cho Dak-On
    - Cho Dak-Man
  - Lok Lan-Gong
  - Lok's Nephew ─── Lai Hip-Chi

- "Hung Gun" Biu ─── Cheung Gung ─── Wong Ting

- "Dai Dong Fung"
  - Tse Gwok-Leung ─── Lao Dat-Sang ("Pao Fa Lien")
  - Tse Gwok-Cheung

- Others…

122

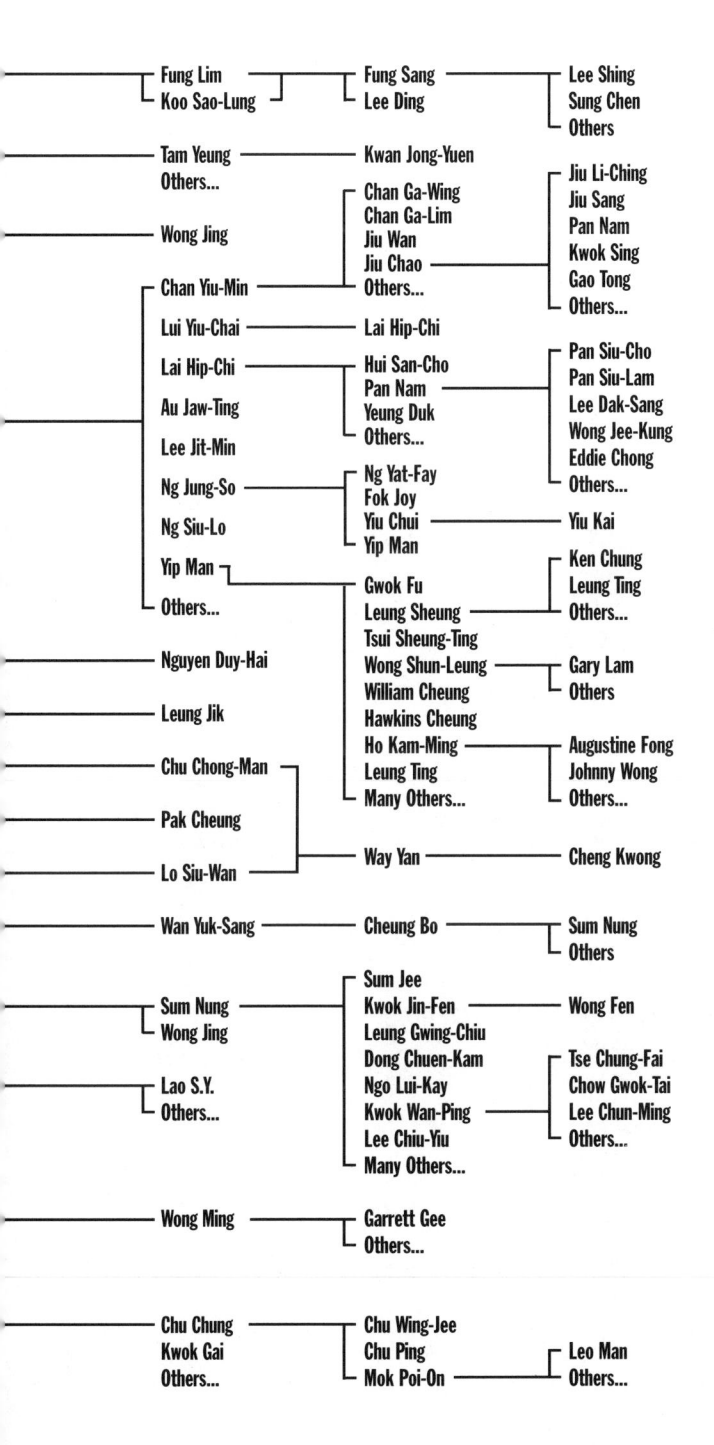

- Fung Lim
- Koo Sao-Lung
  - Fung Sang
  - Lee Ding
    - Lee Shing
    - Sung Chen
    - Others

- Tam Yeung
- Others...
  - Kwan Jong-Yuen

- Wong Jing

- Chan Yiu-Min
  - Chan Ga-Wing
  - Chan Ga-Lim
  - Jiu Wan
  - Jiu Chao
  - Others...
    - Jiu Li-Ching
    - Jiu Sang
    - Pan Nam
    - Kwok Sing
    - Gao Tong
    - Others...

- Lui Yiu-Chai
  - Lai Hip-Chi

- Lai Hip-Chi
  - Hui San-Cho
  - Pan Nam
  - Yeung Duk
  - Others...
    - Pan Siu-Cho
    - Pan Siu-Lam
    - Lee Dak-Sang
    - Wong Jee-Kung
    - Eddie Chong
    - Others...

- Au Jaw-Ting

- Lee Jit-Min

- Ng Jung-So
  - Ng Yat-Fay
  - Fok Joy
  - Yiu Chui — Yiu Kai
  - Yip Man

- Ng Siu-Lo

- Yip Man
- Others...
  - Gwok Fu
  - Leung Sheung
  - Tsui Sheung-Ting
  - Wong Shun-Leung
  - William Cheung
  - Hawkins Cheung
  - Ho Kam-Ming
  - Leung Ting
  - Many Others...
    - Ken Chung
    - Leung Ting
    - Others...
    - Gary Lam
    - Others
    - Augustine Fong
    - Johnny Wong
    - Others...

- Nguyen Duy-Hai

- Leung Jik

- Chu Chong-Man

- Pak Cheung

- Lo Siu-Wan
  - Way Yan — Cheng Kwong

- Wan Yuk-Sang
  - Cheung Bo
    - Sum Nung
    - Others

- Sum Nung
- Wong Jing
  - Sum Jee
  - Kwok Jin-Fen — Wong Fen
  - Leung Gwing-Chiu
  - Dong Chuen-Kam
  - Ngo Lui-Kay
  - Kwok Wan-Ping
  - Lee Chiu-Yiu
  - Many Others...
    - Tse Chung-Fai
    - Chow Gwok-Tai
    - Lee Chun-Ming
    - Others...

- Lao S.Y.
- Others...

- Wong Ming
  - Garrett Gee
  - Others...

- Chu Chung
- Kwok Gai
- Others...
  - Chu Wing-Jee
  - Chu Ping
  - Mok Poi-On
    - Leo Man
    - Others...

123

Glossary

詞彙表

The following glossary will cover the names and terminology (styles, forms, movements, and concepts) found in this book and used by the various branches of Wing Chun kuen. Entries are presented in romanized Cantonese, pinyin, and traditional Chinese characters and with English translations where necessary.

PEOPLE AND ORGANIZATIONS

Au Jaw-Ting (Ou Fangting) 區仿庭
Au Hong (Ou Kang) 區康
Au Si (Ou Shi) 區仕
Baat Hop Wui Goon (Bahehuiguan) 八合會館 Eight Harmony Union
Bak Mei Tao Yan (Baimei Daoren) 白眉道人 "White Eyebrow", taoist
Chan Ga-Chai (Chen Jiaji) 陳家濟
Chan Ga-Lim (Chen Jialian) 陳家廉
Chan Ga-Wing (Chen Jiarong) 陳家榮
Chan Hui (Chen Kai) 陳開
Chan Shing (Chen Cheng) 陳成 Chris Chan
Chan Wah-Shun (Chen Huashun) 陳華
Chan Yiu-Min (Chen Rumian) 陳汝棉
Cheung Bo (Zhang Bao) 張保
Cheung Chuk-Hing (Zhang Zhuoqing) 張卓慶 William Cheung
Cheung Gung (Zhang Gong) 張弓

"Cheung Gwun Wong" ("Changgun Wang") 長棍王 "King of the Long Pole"
Cheung Hok-Kin (Zhang Xuejian) 張學健 Hawkins Cheung
Cheung Ng (Zhang Wu) 張五
Cho Dak-Man (Cao Dewen) 曹德文
Cho Dak-On (Cao Dean) 曹德安
Cho Dak-Sang (Cao Desheng) 曹德生
Chong Yin-Cheung (Zhuang Xuanxiang) 莊鉉翔 Eddie Chong
Chow Kwong-Yiu (Zhou Guangyu) 周光裕
Chow Sai (Zhou Xi) 周細
Chu Chong (Zhu Zhong) 朱忠
Chu Chong-Man (Zhu Songmin) 朱頌民
Chu Gwok-Yiu (Zhu GuoYao) 朱國
Chu King-Hung (Zhu Jingxiong) 朱競雄 Garrett Gee
Chu Wing-Jee (Zhu Rongzhi) 朱榮枝
"Chu Yuk" Kwai ("Zhurou" Gui) 豬肉桂 "Butcher" Kwai
Chung Man-Lin (Zhong Wannian) 鍾萬年 Ken Chung
"Chut Sang Gwun Wong" ("Qisheng Gunwang") 七省棍王 "King of the Pole of Seven Provinces"
"Dai Dong Fung" ("Dadongfeng") 大東風 "Great East Wind"
"Dai Fa Min" Kam ("Dahuamian" Jin) 大花面錦 "Painted Face" Kam
"Dai San" Siu ("Dashan" Shu) 大山樹
"Dao Po" Chai ("Doupi" Ji) 豆皮濟 "Pock Skin" Chai
"Do Ngan" Shun ("Daoyan" Shun) 道眼順 "Shifty Eyes" Shun
Dong Chuen-Kam (Dong Quanjin) 董全錦
"Fa Jee" Ming ("Huazhi" Ming) 花志明 "Flower Mark" Ming
Fok Bo-Chuen (Huo Baoquan) 霍保全
Fok Joy (Huo Zhu) 霍珠
Fong Chi-Wing (Fang Zhirong) 方致榮 Augustine Fong
Fong Sai-Yuk (Fang Shiyu) 方世玉
Fung Do-Duk (Feng Daode) 馮道德
Fung Hon (Feng Han) 馮漢 Stewart Fung
Fung Lim (Feng Lian) 馮廉
Fung Sang (Feng Sheng) 馮生

Fung Siu-Ching (Feng Shaoqing) 馮少青
Fung Ting (Feng Ting) 馮挺
Fung Wah (Feng Hua) 馮華
"Gao Lo" Chung ("Gaolao" Zhong) 高佬忠 "Tall Man" Chung
Gao Tong (Gao Tang) 高堂
"Hak Min" Nam ("Heimian" Nan) 黑面南 "Black Face" Nam
Ho Han-Lui (He Hanlu) 何漢侶
Ho Kam-Ming (He Jinge) 何金鉻
Hui Sam-Joy (Xu Sanzhu) 許三硃
Hung Fa Wui Goon (Honghuahuiguan) 紅花會館 Red Flower Union
Hung Fook (Kong Fu) 孔福
"Hung Gun" Biu ("Hongjin" Biao) 紅巾彪 "Red Bandanna" Biu
Hung Gwun Wui (Honggunhui) 紅棍會 Red Pole Society
Hung Mun (Kong Man) 孔滿
Hung Mun Wui (Hongmenhui) 紅門會 Hung Mun Society
Hung Suen Hay Ban (Hongchuan Xiban) 紅船戲班 Red Junk Opera Company
Jan Sin-Sang (Zan Xiansheng) 贊先生 Mr. Jan
Jee Shim Sim Si (Zhi Shan Chanshi) 至善禪師 Jee Shim Chan (Buddhist) Teacher
"Jiao-Chin" Wah ("Zhaoqian" Hua) 找錢華 "Moneychanger" Wah
Jiu Chao (Zhao Jiu) 招就
Jiu Ching (Zhao Cheng) 招澄
Jiu Sang (Zhao Song) 招崧
Jiu Wan (Zhao Yun) 招允
Kan Wah-Chit (Jian Huajie) 簡華捷 Victor Kan
Koo Sang (Gu Sheng) 古生
Koo Siu-Lung (Gu Zhaolong) 古兆龍
Kwan Jong-Yuen (Guan Juangyuan) 關椿元
Kwok Fu (Guo Fu) 郭富
Kwok Gai (Guo Jia) 郭佳
Kwok Jin-Fen (Guo Junfen) 郭俊芬
Kwok Sing (Guo Cheng) 郭成
Kwok Wan-Ping (Guo Yunping) 郭運平

Kwong Din-Hing (Guang Dianqing) 廣殿卿
Lai Fook-Shun (Li Fushun) 黎福孫
Lai Hip-Chi (Li Xiechi) 黎協池
Lai Yeung-Yin (Li Yangqiao) 黎仰翹
Lai Ying (Li Ying) 黎英
Lao Dat-Sang (Liu Dasheng) 劉達生
Lao Man-Kay (Liu Minqi) 劉民祺
Lee Chi-Yiu (Li Zhiyao) 李志耀
Lee Dak-Sang (Liu Desheng) 李德生
Lee Ding (Li Ding) 李丁
Lee Jit-Man (Li Zhewen) 李哲文
Lee Man (Li Min) 李民
Lee Man-Mao (Li Wenmao) 李文茂
Lee Shing (Li Sheng) 李勝
Lee Siu-Long (Li Xiaolong) 李小龍 Bruce Lee
Leung Bak Cheung (Liang Bozhang) 梁伯長
Leung Bik (Liang Bi) 梁壁
Leung Bok-Tao (Liang Bochou) 梁博儔
Leung Chong-Ting (Liang Cangting) 梁滄亭
Leung Chun (Liang Chun) 梁春
Leung Dai-Chiu (Leung Dazhou) 梁大釗
Leung Jan (Liang Zan) 梁贊
Leung Jik (Liang Zhi) 梁植
Leung Kay (Liang Qi) 梁奇
Leung Keung (Liang Quan) 梁權
Leung Kwok-Keung (Liang Guoqiang) 梁國強
Leung Lan-Kwai (Liang Langui) 梁蘭桂
Leung Sheung (Liang Xiang) 梁相
Leung Ting (Liang Ting) 梁挺
Leung Yan (Liang En) 梁恩
Leung Yee-Tai (Liang Erdi) 梁二娣
Lo Kwai (Lu Gui) 盧桂
Lo Man-Gung (Luo Wangong) 羅晚恭
Lo Man-Kam (Lu Wenjin) 盧文錦
Lok Lan-Gong (Lu Langong) 陸蘭宮

Lok Yiu (Luo Yao) 駱耀
Lui Yiu-Chai (Lei Ruji) 雷汝濟
Lun Fao (Lun Huo) 倫伙
Lun Gai (Lun Jie) 倫佳
Ma Jung-Yiu (Ma Zhongru) 馬仲如
Ma Ning-Yee (Ma Ninger) 馬寧兒
"Mai Gai" Wong ("Mi Ji" Huang) 米機黃 "Rice Machine" Wong
Miu Hin (Miao Xian) 苗顯
Miu Shun (Miao Shun) 苗順
Miu Tsui-Fa (Miu Jiahua) 苗筴花
Mok Poi-On (Mo Peian) 莫沛安
Moy Yat (Mei Yi) 梅逸
"Muk Yan" Wah ("Muren" Hua) 木人華
Ng jo (wuzu) 五祖 five elders
Ng Jung-So (Wu Zhongsu) 吳仲素
Ng Mui Si Tai (Wu Mei Shitai) 五枚師太 "Five Plums", nun
Ng Siu-Lo (Wu Xiaolu) 吳小魯
Ng Yat-Fei (Wu Yifei) 吳一飛
Ngo Lui-Kay (Ao Leiqi) 敖磊奇
Pan Nam (Peng Nan) 彭南
Pan Siu-Cho (Peng Shuhan) 彭樹漢
Pan Siu-Lam (Peng Shulin) 彭樹霖
"Pao Fa Lien" ("Paohua Lian") 刨花蓮 "Wood-Planer Lien"
Sum Jee (Cen Zhi) 岑芝
Sum Nung (Cen Neng) 岑能
Sun Fook-Chung (Sun Fucheng) 孫福全
Sun Wah (Xin Hua) 新華
Tam Yeung (Tan Yang) 譚陽
Tien Dei Wui (Tiandihui) 天地會 Heaven and Earth Society
Tse Gwok-Cheung (Xie Guozhang) 謝國樟
Tse Gwok-Leung (Xie Guoliang) 謝國梁
Tsui Seung-Tin (Xu Shangtian) 徐尚田
Wan Yuk-Sang (Wei Yusheng) 韋玉生
"Wing Chun Wong" ("Yongchunwang") 詠春王 "King of Wing Chun"

Wong Jee-Keung (Huang Zhiqiang) 黃志強
Wong Jing (Huang Zhen) 黃貞
Wong Kiu (Wang Qiao) 王喬
Wong "Lao Fu" (Wang "Laohu") 王老虎 "Old Tiger" Wong
Wong Ming (Wang Ming) 王明
Wong Shun-Leung (Huang Chunliang) 黃淳樑
Wong Ting (Wang Ting) 王挺
Wong Wah-Bo (Huang Huabao) 黃華寶
Wong Wah-Sum (Huang Huasan) 黃華三
Yat Chum Dai Si (Yi Chen Dashi) 一塵大師 "Speck of Dust", monk
Yat Chum Um Jee (Yi Chen Anzhu) 一塵菴主 "Speck of Dust", founder of convent
Yee "Gung" (Yan "Gong") 嚴公 "Grandfather" Yee
Yeung Biu (Yang Biao) 陽彪 Robert Yeung
Yeung Dak (Yang De) 陽德
Yeung Sang (Yang Sheng) 陽生
Yik Ying (Yi Ying) 易英
Yim Man (Yan Wen) 嚴文
Yim Wing-Chun (Yan Yongchun) 嚴詠春
Yim Yee (Yan Er) 嚴二
Yim Sei (Yan Si) 嚴四
Yin Li-Chung (Xian Lizhang) 賢麗章
Yip Ching (Ye Zheng) 葉正
Yip Chun (Ye Zhun) 葉凖
Yip Kam (Ye Jin) 葉錦
Yip Kin (Ye Jian) 葉堅
Yip Man (Ye Wen) 葉問
Yip Man-Sun (Ye Mingshen) 葉名深
Yiu Chui (Yao Cai) 姚才
Yiu Kai (Yao Qi) 姚祺
Yuen Chai-Wan (Ruan Jiyun) 阮濟云
Yuen Kay-San (Ruan Qishan) 阮奇山
Yuen "Lo-Jia" (Ruan "Laozha") 阮老楂 Yuen "The Fifth"

STYLES, FORMS, MOVEMENTS, AND EXERCISES

At yiu (yayao) 壓腰 pressing the waist
Baat gwa bo 八卦步 eight triagrams step
Baat gwa lung na (bagua longna) 八卦龍拿 eight direction dragon grab
Baat gwa sum (baguaxin) 八卦心 eight trigrams center
Baat sik dan da (bashi danda) 八式單打 eight form single hit
Bai jong (baizhuang) 擺樁 assume post
Bak hok chang sa (baihe chansha) 白鶴鏟沙 white crane shoveling sand
Bak hok kuen (baihequan) 白鶴拳 white crane boxing
Bak hok kum wu (baihe qin hu) 白鶴擒狐 white crane catches the fox
Bak hok tan sui (baihe tan shui) 白鶴攤水 white crane explores water
Bak Mei pai (Baimeipai) 白眉派 White Eyebrow's style
Bao pai jeung (baopaizhang) 抱排掌 shield holding palms
Bik bong (bibang) 逼膀 pressing wing
Bik ma (bima) 逼馬 pressing stance
Bien chui (bianchui) 鞭錘 whipping punch
Bien kuen (bianquan) 鞭拳 whipping fist
Biu jee (biaozhi) 標指 darting fingers
Biu sao (biaosao) 標手 darting arm
Bong sao (bangshou) 膀手 wing arm
Boon tan bong (bantanbang) 半攤膀 half-dispersing, half-wing
Chai mei gwun (qimeigun) 齊眉棍 eyebrow level pole
Chang jeung (chanzhang) 鏟掌 shovel palm
Chang gerk (chanjiao) 鏟腳 shovel kick
Chao chui (chouchui) 抽錘 bouncing punch
Charp chui (chachui) 插錘 piercing punch
Charp sao (chashou) 插錘 piercing arm
Cheung lung tan yue (changlong tan yue) 長龍探月 long dragon explores the moon
Cheung sam bo (zhangshanbu) 長衫步 long-robe steps
Chi gerk (chijiao) 黐腳 sticking legs

Chi gwun (chigun) 黐棍 sticking pole

Chi sao (chishou) 黐手 sticking arms

Chit jeung (qie zhang) 切掌 slice

Chiu mien jui ying gwun (chaomian zhuixing gun) 朝面追形棍 facing and chasing posture pole

Chuen sum gerk (chuanxinjiao) 穿心腳 center piercing kick

Chum kiu (chenqiao) 沉橋 sinking bridge

Chum kiu (xunqiao) 尋橋 seeking bridge

Chum kiu ma (xumqiaoma) 尋橋馬 bridge seeking stance

Chum sao (chenshou) 沉手 sinking hands

Chun chiu dai do (chunqiu dadao) 春秋大刀 spring and autumn big knives

Chung chui (chongchui) 衝錘 thrusting punch

Chung jeung (chongzhang) 衝掌 thrusting palm

Chut lun (qilun) 七輪 seven wheels

Chut sing bo (qixingbu) 七星步 seven star step

Cup da sao (qiadashou) 洽打手 covering and hitting hand

Da san jong (dasanzhuang) 打散樁 separate hitting dummy

Dai bong (dabang) 大膀 big wing

Dai fa kuen (dahuaquan) 大花拳 big flower fist

Dai fook fu (dafuhu) 大伏虎 big subduing the tiger

Dai jeung (dizhang) 氐掌 low palm

Dai pa (daba) 大扒 trident

Dan chi sao (danchishou) 單黐手 single sticking arms

Dao jong (daozhuang) 刀樁 knife dummy

Ding gerk (dingjiao) 釘腳 nailing kick

Ding jeung 釘掌 nailing palms

Dip jeung (diezhang) 蝶掌 butterfly palm

Diu ma (diaoma) 吊馬 hanging stance

Do lung chui (dulongchui) 獨龍錘 single dragon punch

Duen kiu (duanqiao) 短橋 short bridge

Dui sao (duoshou) 剁手 chopping hand

Fa kuen (huaquan) 花拳 variegated fist

Fan cup chui (fanqiachui) 反洽錘 flipping covering punch (uppercut)

Fao jeung (fuzhang) 浮掌 floating palm
Fong ngan chui (fengyanchui) 鳳眼錘 phoenix eye punch
Fook fu dai pa (fuhu daba) 伏虎大扒 subdue tiger big trident
Fook fu jang (fuhuzhou) 伏虎肘 subdue tiger elbows
Fook fu kuen (fuhuquan) 伏虎拳 subdue tiger fist
Fook sao (fushou) 伏手 controlling arm
Fu hok seung ying kuen (hu he shuangxingquan) 虎鶴雙形拳
    tiger crane twin form fist
Fu jow (huzhao) 虎爪 tiger claw
Fu mei (humei) 虎尾 tiger's tail
Fu mei gerk (huweijiao) 虎尾腳 tiger tail kick
Fut jeung (fozhang) 佛掌 Buddha palm
Fut sao (foshou) 佛手 Buddha hand
Gang sao (jingshou) 經手 crossing arm
Gaun sao (gengshou) 耕手 cultivating hand
Gao dai jeung (gaodizhang) 高底掌 high and low palms
Gao san (jiushen) 救身 saving body
Gerk jong (jiaozhuang) 腳樁 kicking dummy
Gong hung (kuoxiong) 擴胸 expanding chest
Gong jong (gangzhuang) 剛樁 hard dummy
Gulao sei sup dim Wing Chun (Gulao Sishidian Yongchunquan)
    古勞四十點詠春拳 Gulao forty point Wing-Chun boxing
Gum gong jeung (jingangzhang) 金剛掌 diamond (Buddhist) palms
Gum sao (jinshou) 禁手 pinning hand
Gung jee ma (gongzima) 弓字馬 bow shape stance
Gwa chui (Guachui) 掛錘 hanging punch (back-fist)
Gwa lung jeung (gualongzhang) 掛龍掌 hanging dragon palm
Gwai ma chui (guimachui) 跪馬錘 kneeling stance punch
Gwok ma (juema) 角馬 angle stance
Gwun jong (gunzhuang) 棍樁 pole dummy
Hay sup (qixi) 起膝 rising knee
Hei gung (qigong) 氣功 breath/intrinsic energy work
Hok bong (hebang) 鶴膀 crane wing
Hok ying sao bo (hexingshoubo) 鶴形手步 crane shape hand step
Hong jong (kongzhuang) 空樁 air dummy

Huen bo (juanbu) 圈步 circling step
Huen sao (juanshou) 圈手 circling arms
Hung ga kuen (Hongjiaquan) 洪家拳 Hung family boxing
Hung Suen Wing Chun kuen 紅船詠春拳 Red Boat Praise
    Spring boxing
Hung Suen Hay Ban Wing Chun 紅船戲班詠春拳 Red Boat
    Opera Praise Spring boxing
Hut yee sao (qiershou) 乞兒手 beggar's hand
Jee ng chui (ziwuchui) 子午錘 meridian punch
Jee ng ma (ziwuma) 子午馬 meridian stance
Jee Shim Wing Chun kuen (Zhi Shan Yongchunquan) 至善禪師
    Jee Shim's Always Spring boxing
Jik chung chui (zhichongchui) 直衝錘 straight thrusting punch
Jin chui (jianchui) 箭錘 arrow punch
Jin jeung (jinzhang) 箭掌 arrow palm
Jin kuen (jinquan) 箭拳 arrow fist
Jong kuen (zhuangquan) 樁拳 dummy fist
Jow sao (zhaosao) 爪手 clawing hand
Juen bo (zhuanbu) 轉步 turning step
Juen ma (zhuanma) 轉馬 turning stance
Jui da (zhuida) 追打 chasing hitting
Jui kuen (zuiquan) 醉拳 drunken boxing
Juk da (ceda) 側打 slanting strike
Juk jong (zhuzhuang) 竹樁 bamboo dummy
Juk kiu (ceqiao) 側橋 slanting bridge
Juk san (ceshen) 側身 side body
Jung bong (zhongbang) 中膀 middle wing
Kam jang (gaizhou) 蓋肘 covering elbow
Kam sao (gaishou) 蓋手 covering hand
Kao bo (koubu) 搆步 hooking step
Kao geng sao (koujingshou) 扣頸手 neck detaining arm
Kao sao (koushou) 扣手 detaining arm
Kei jang (zhanzhou) 站手 standing elbow
Keung jee chui (jiangzichui) 姜字錘 ginger shape punch
Kum na (qinna) 擒拿 seizing and holding

Kwan do (Guan dao) 關刀 Kwan's knife
Kwun sao (kunshou) 捆手 binding arm
Lan sao (lanshou) 欄手 barring arm
Lao sao (liushou) 溜手 slipping hand
Lao yip seung do (liuye shuangdao) 柳葉雙刀 willow leaf
    double knives
Lien wan chui (lianhuanchui) 連環錘 linked chain punch
Lien wan fai jeung (lianhuan kuaizhang) 連環快掌 linked fast palms
Lien wan kao da (lianhuan kouda) 連環扣打 continuous capture hit
Liu yum gerk (liaoyinjiao) 撩陰腳 lifting yin kick
Loi lim yum yeung cheung (li lian yin yang zhang) 里簾陰陽掌
    inside outside yin and yang palms
Loi kiu (liqiao) 里橋 double bridges
Lop sao (lieshou) 擸手 grasping arm
Luk dim boon gwun (liudianbangun) 六點半棍 six and a half
    point pole
Luk sao (lushou) 碌手 rolling hands
Lung Ying Kuen (longxingquan) 龍形拳 Dragon shape boxing
Mai sang jong (maishengzhuang) 埋生椿 live dummy
Malaysia Wing Chun kuen (Malaixiya Yongchunquan)
    馬來西亞永春拳 Malaysian Always Spring boxing
Mei lui chuen jaam (meinu chuanzhen) 美女穿針 fair lady
    threads needles
Mo yieng gerk (wuyingjiao) 無影腳 shadowless kick
Mo sut (wushu) 武術 martial arts
Mor poon seung do (mopan shuangdao) 磨盤雙刀 millstone
    double knife
Mui fa baat gwa (meihua bagua) 枚花八卦 plum blossom
    eight trigrams
Mui fa cheung (meihuaqiang) 枚花槍 plum blossom spear
Mui fa jong (Meihuazhuang) 枚花椿 plum flower dummy
Mui fa kuen (meihuaquan) 枚花拳 plum flower boxing
Muk yan jong (murenzhuang) 木人椿 wooden dummy
Mun sao (wenshou) 問手 asking hand

Nam Yeung Wing Chun kuen (Nanyang Yongchunquan) 南洋詠春
    South East Asian Wing-Chun boxing
Ng jee mui hei gung (wuzhimei qigong) 五指枚氣功 five petal
    plum qigong
Ng Mui pai (Wumeipai) 五枚派 Five Plum's style
Ngok ga kuen (Yuejiaquan) 岳家拳 Ngok family boxing
Ng ying hei gung (wuxing qigong) 五形氣功 five shape
    (animal) qigong
Ng ying kuen (wuxingquan) 五形拳 five shape boxing
Ngoi lop (wailie) 外捯 outside grasp
Ngoi dap (waida) 外搭 outside join
Ngoi jong (waizhuang) 外樁 outside dummy
Ngoi lim sao (wailianshou) 外鐮手 outside sickle hand
Noi lop (neilie) 內捯 inside grasp
Noi dap (neida) 內搭 inside join
Noi jong (neizhuang) 內樁 inside dummy
Noi lim sao (neilianshou) 內鐮手 inside sickle hand
Pai jang (pizhou) 批肘 hacking elbows
Pak sao (paishou) 拍手 slapping hand
Pan Nam Wing Chun kuen (Peng Nan Yongchunquan)
    彭南永春拳 Pan Nam's Always Spring boxing
Pao bong (paobang) 拋膀 throwing wing
Pao chui (paochui) 炮錘 cannon punch
Pao Fa Lien Wing Chun kuen (Paohua Lian Yongchunquan)
    刨花蓮永春拳 Wood-Planer Lien's Always Spring boxing
Pien chui (pianchui) 偏錘 side punch
Pien jeung (pianzhang) 偏掌 slant palm
Pien san dip jeung (pianshen diezhang) 偏身蝶掌 side body
    butterfly palm
Pien san jeung (pianshenzhang) 偏身掌 slant body palm
Pien san ma (pianshenma) 偏身馬 side body stance
Pien san Wing Chun kuen (pianshen Yongchunquan) 偏身詠春拳
    side body Wing-Chun boxing
Ping lan sao (pinlanshou) 平欄手 level obstruction hand
Po jung sao (pochongshou) 破中手 center cleaving arm

Pok yic jeung (puyizhang) 扑翼掌 flapping wing palm
Poon sao (panshou) 盤手 rolling hands
Saat jeung (shazhang) 殺掌 killing palm
Saat kiu (shaqiao) 殺橋 killing bridge
Sae ying sao (shexingshou) 蛇形手 snake shape hand
Sae ying kuen (shexingquan) 蛇形拳 snake shape boxing
Sam bai fut (sanbeifo) 三拜佛 three bows to buddha
Sam dim boon gwun (sandianbangun) 三點半棍 three and a half point pole
Sam gwok ma (sanjuema) 三角馬 triangle step
Sam jin chui (sanjianchiu) 三箭錘 three arrow blows
Sam juen jeung (sanzhuanzhang) 三轉掌 three turning palms
Sam moon kuen (sanmenquan) 三門拳 three gates fist
Sam sing chui (sanxingchui) 三星錘 three star punch
Sam sing gerk (sanxingjiao) 三星腳 three star kick
Sam sing jong (sanxingzhuang) 三星樁 three star dummy
San sao (sanshou) 散手 separate hands
Sao gerk (saojiao) 掃腳 sweeping kick
Sei ping ma (sipingma) 四平馬 quadrilateral level stance
Sei mun (simen) 四門 four gates
Sei sup dim (sishidian) 四十點 forty points
Seung chi sao (shuangchishou) 雙黐手 double sticking arms
Seung chum do (shuangchendo) 雙沉刀 double sinking knives
Seung huen sao (shuangjuanshou) 雙圈手 double circling arms
Seung lung (shuanglong) 雙龍 double dragons
Sin mien gwun (shanmiangun) 扇面棍 fanning pole
Siu baat gwa (xiaobagua) 小八卦 little eight trigrams
Siu fa kuen (xiaohuaquan) 小花拳 small flower fist
Siu fook fu (xiaofuhu) 小伏虎 small subduing the tiger
Siu lien tao (xiaoliantou) 小練頭 little first training
Siu lung gim (shulangjian) 曹郎劍 scholar's sword
Siu mui fa (xiaomeihua) 小梅花 little plum flower
Siu nim tao (xiaoniantou) 小念頭 little idea
Siu ng ying (xiaowuxing) 小五形 small five elements
Siu poon sao (xiopanshou) 小盤手 small rolling hands

Sui da (suida) 隨打 random hitting
Sun hei (shunqi) 順氣 yielding breath
Sun hei gwai yuen (shenqiguiyuan) 腎氣歸元 kidney breathing invigoration
Sup baat jin kuen (shiba jianquan) 十八箭拳 eighteen arrow fist
Sup jee (shizi) 十字 "十" character
Sup jee sao (shizishou) 十字手 "十" character arm
Sup sam yei yun bin (shisan jieyebian) 十三節野鞭 thirteen section whip
Sup yee sik (shiershi) 十二式 twelve forms
Sup yee san sao (shier sanshou) 十二散手 twelve separate hands
Sut gow (shuaijiao) 摔跤 wrestling
Tai gik kuen (Taijiquan) 太極 great ultimate boxing
Tan gung gerk (tangongjiao) 彈功腳 spring leg
Tan sao (tansho) 攤手 spread-out arm
Tat sao (tashou) 撻手 whipping hand
Tiet pao jang (tiebaozhou) 鐵包肘 iron elbow
Tiet sin kuen (tiexianquan) 鐵線拳 iron wire fist
Tok sao (tuoshou) 托手 lifting hand
Tong long kuen (tanglangquan) 螳螂 preying mantis boxing
Tui sao (tuishou) 推手 pushing arms
Tun sao (tunshou) 吞手 swallowing arm
Tut sao (tuoshou) 脫手 freeing hand
Wan wun yiu tiet ban kiu (huanhunyao tiebanqiao) 還魂腰鐵板橋 emergency waist bend and iron bridge
Wang ding gerk (hengdingjiao) 橫釘腳 side nailing kick
Wang ma (hengma) 橫馬 side stance
Wing chun kuen (yongchunquan) 永春拳 always spring boxing
Wing Chun kuen (Yongchunquan) 詠春拳 Praise Spring boxing
Wing Chun sup yat sao (Yongchun shiyishou) 永春十一手 Wing Chun eleven hands
Wu dip jeung (hudiezhang) 蝴蝶掌 butterfly palms
Wu dip seung do (hudie shuangdao) 蝴蝶雙刀 double butterfly knives

Wu dip seung fei jeung (hudie shuang feizhang) 蝴蝶雙飛掌
 butterfly flying double palms
Yan jee do (renzidao) 人字刀 "人" character knives
Yao jong (rouzhuang) 柔樁 soft dummy
Yat jee chung chui (rizichongchui) 日子衝錘 "日" character
 thrusting punch
Yee jee kim yeung ma (erzi qianyang ma) 二字箝羊馬
 "二" character pinching goat stance
Yee jee kim yeung ma (erzi qianyang ma) 二字箝陽馬
 "二" character yang pressing stance
Yee jee ma (erzima) 二字馬 "二" character stance
Yee jee seung dao (erzishuangdao) 二字雙刀 "二" character
 double knives
Yee ma (yi ma) 移馬 moving stance
Ying jow (yingzhao) 鷹爪 eagle claw
Ying jow pai (Yingzhaopai) 鷹爪派 eagle claw style
Yip Man Wing Chun kuen (Ye Wen Yongchunquan) 葉問詠春拳
 Yip Man's Praise Spring boxing
Yiu Kai Wing Chun kuen (Yao Qi Yongchuquan) 姚祺詠春拳
 Yiu Kai's Wing Chun boxing
Yuen Kay-San Wing Chun kuen (Ruan Qishan Yongchunquan)
 阮奇山詠春拳 Yuen Kay-San's Praise Spring boxing
Yuet Nam Wing Chun kuen (Yuenan Yongchunquan) 越南詠春拳
 Vietnamese Praise Spring boxing
Yum yeung baat gwa gwun (yin yang bagua gun) 陰陽八卦棍
 yin yang eight trigram pole

CONCEPTS AND SAYINGS

Bik ging (bijing) 逼勁 pressing power
Bien jung sin (bianzhongxian) 變中線 centerline adjusting
Biu (biao) 鏢 dart
Bo lay tao, dao fu san, tiet kiu sao (bolitou, doufushen, tieqiaoshou)
 玻璃頭, 豆腐身, 鐵橋手 glass head, bean-curd body
 iron bridges
Chai (cai) 采 stamp

Chi (chi) 黐 stick

Chi sao mo lien fa sik (chishou wulian huashi) 黐手無練花式 no flowery techniques practiced during sticking arms

Chit (jie) 切 slice

Chuen (cun) 寸 inch

Chuen Ging (cunjing) 寸勁 inch power

Chum (chen) 沉 sink

Da sao jik siu sao (dashou ji xiaoshou) 打手即消手 striking hand is defending hand

Do mo seung faat (dao wushuangfa) 刀無雙法 knife techniques are not repeated

Dap (da) 搭 join

Dim (dian) 點 point

Dong (dang) 盪 swing

Dui gang yiu jong tao (duijing yu zhuang qiu) 對鏡與樁求 face a mirror and dummy to aid in this pursuit

Faat mun (famen) 法門 methodology

Fan Ching fook Ming (fan Qing fu Ming) 反清复明 Overthrow the Qing dynasty, return the Ming dynasty

Fao (fu) 浮 rise

Fa chuk dui sao chi (huachai dui shouchi) 化拆對手黐 explore changes by sticking with a partner

Fung lut jik jong (fengshuai zhichong) 逢甩直沖 charge straight when free

Gerk mo hui faat 腳無虛發 kick does not miss

Gong yao ping yung (gangrou bingyong) 剛柔幷用 hard and soft combine in use

Got (ge) 割 cut down

Gwun mo leung heung (gun wuliangsheng) 棍無兩聲 pole has not two sounds

Jeet (jie) 截 intercept

Jui (sui) 隨 follow

Jum (zhen) 針 needle

Jung sien dui ying (zhongxian duiying) 中線對形 centerline facing shape

Kit (jie) 揭 deflect

Kuen ku (quanjue) 拳訣 boxing rhymed formulae

Kuen yao sum faat (quanyouxinfa) 拳由心發 boxing originates from the heart

Lao (lou) 漏 leak

Lien juk bat ting lao (lianxu butingliu) 連續不停留 continue without stopping or staying

Lien siu dai da (lianxiao daida) 連消帶打 link defending and attacking

Liu (liao) 撩 stir

Lik chui jee gok chuen (lisuizhijuezhuan) 力隨知覺轉 strength is aware, it follows and changes with feeling

Lui lao hui soong (lailiu qusong) 來留去送 keep what comes send off what goes

Lui saat chak (laijuezhe) 來決折 you may not prevail

Lut sao jik chung (shuaishou zhichong) 甩手直衝 hands disengage, charge forward

Mo (mo) 摸 feel

Mo jiu mo chak (wuzhao wuzhe) 無招無折 No (fixed) technique, no resistance

Mo keung da (wuqiangda) 無強打 don't force your strike

Mo luen da (moluanda) 無亂打 don't waste your strike

Mo ying da yieng (wuxing daying) 無形打影 no form, strike shadow

Na (nian) 黏 adhere

Ngao (gou) 鉤 hook

Saat (sha) 刹 brake

Sao chi sao mo dei jo (shouchishou wudizou) 手黐手無地走 when hands stick to hands, there is nowhere to go.

Sao gerk seung siu, mo jit jiu (shoujiaoxiangxiao, wujuezhao) 手腳相消,無絕招 hand and feet defend accordingly no unstoppable maneuvers

Sao lao jung sien (shouliuzhongxian) 手留中線 hand remains in the centerline

Sup Yee Faat (shier fa) 十二法 twelve methods

Tarn (tan) 彈 spring

Tao (tu) 吐 spit
Tao (tou) 偷 steal
Tek (ti) 踢 kick
Tong (tang) 搪 ward-off
Tong (tang) 熨 press
Tai (ti) 提 raise
Tui (tui) 推 push
Tun (tun) 吞 swallow
Wai seung chak (weishangzhe) 為上折 you prevail every time
Wing yun chi jee; mo mong Hon juk; Dai dei wui chun (yongyinshizhi; wuwang Hanzu dadihuichun) 永言失志, 毋忘漢族, 大地回春 always speak with determination; don't forget the Han nation again will return spring
Wun (yun) 運 circle
Yao ying da ying (youxing daxing) 有形打形 When you see form, strike form
Yat jiu yat chak (yizhao yizhe) 一招一折 one block, one strike
Yee ching jai dong (yijing zhidong) 以靜制動 use stillness to overcome movement
Yee yao jai gong (yirou zhigang) 以柔制剛 use soft to overcome hard
Yee yat tui lo (yiyi dailao) 以逸待勞 use rest to overcome fatigue
Yiu jee (yaozhi) 要旨 important ideas
Yiu ku (Yaojue) 要訣 important rhymed formulae

About The Authors

In 1995, Y. Wu and Rene Ritchie met through the Internet Wing Chun Mailing List. They soon began discussing Wing Chun, finding much common ground and opportunity for exchange. At about the same time, Rene Ritchie began publishing his Wing Chun Archives site on the World Wide Web. In late 1995, Robert Chu and Rene Ritchie made contact through Ritchie's Yuen Kay-San Wing Chun kuen Homepage, and a similar dialog began. As work progressed on the Wing Chun Archives site, and the material began to solidify, it was realized that what was often considered conflicting information was, in fact, complementary. It soon became apparent that the information could be of great interest to the larger Wing Chun community. At Y. Wu's suggestion, work on *Complete Wing Chun* began in earnest. As Robert Chu, Y. Wu, and Rene Ritchie all shared a similar passion for Wing Chun kuen and a keen desire to preserve its history and methods, it was only natural that they collaborate on the book. Work was completed almost entirely over the Internet via e-mail and by fax and phone. Technology allowed the authors to collaborate across three countries and two continents almost instantaneously. It is doubtful that in any time past, or with any other medium of exchange, this work could have been possible.

Robert Chu has been involved in martial arts since 1972, and specializes in Wing Chun kuen. Over the years, he has been fortunate to learn several versions of the art such as the Yip Man style from several prominent instructors, including his current teacher Hawkins Cheung, and the Gu Lao and Yuen Kay-San styles from his good friend and teacher Kwan Jong-Yuen. In addition to his Wing Chun knowledge, Robert Chu has instructor rankings in Hung ga kuen and Lama, is a practitioner of Yang and Sun style taiji, Hebei xingyi and baguazhang, and is a successor to Lui Yon-Sang's fei lung fu mun combat staff system in the United States. Robert Chu has also written many articles as a freelance writer in publications such as *Inside Kung-Fu, Video Review, Wing Chun Viewpoint,* and the *Wing Chun Today* newsletter. He also produces a quarterly newsletter called *Chu's Wing Chun,* for practitioners of his system of Wing Chun kuen. He is currently working on several books including *Chu's Wing Chun Kuen Po, Combat Methods of Wing Chun* (with Gary Lam), and the *Wing Chun Weapons Arts.* Robert Chu lives in California where he practices Chinese medicine including diet, herbology, acupuncture, qigong healing, and tui na.

Y. Wu has been involved in Wing Chun since 1984. He is a practitioner of Nanyang Wing Chun under S. Y. Liu and of Yip Man style Wing Chun under Victor Leow. In addition, Y. Wu is a practitioner of Yang Chienhuo style taijiquan, taiji ruler qigong, baguazhang, and ngok ga kuen. Author of *The Nanyang Wing Chun Primer Vol. 1,* and the forthcoming *The Nanyang Wing Chun Primer Vol. 2 and 3,* Y. Wu lives, works, and practices in Southeast Asia.

Rene Ritchie has been studying the Yuen Kay-San style of Wing Chun under the guidance of Ngo Lui-Kay since 1990. He has written articles for *Martial Arts Masters* magazine and the *Wing Chun Today* newsletter (www.wing-chun-today.com), has created and maintains the www.wingchunkuen.com site on the Internet World Wide Web and is currently working on several forthcoming projects. Rene Ritchie works and practices in Eastern Canada.